EMPLOYEE ASSISTANCE PROGRAMMES

ENDORSEMENTS

Employee Assistance Programmes is a well-written and practical guide to help promote employees' health and wellbeing as part of an integrated talent/human capital management strategy.

Having worked as an HR professional in the public sector for more than 11 years, I have seen health programmes fail due to insufficiencies in areas of ethics such as confidentiality. I was so pleased to see that this book emphasises and outlines the ethical considerations necessary for the implementation of Employee Assistance Programmes. In addition, it also highlights the importance of developing comprehensive Employee Assistance Programme policies that are in line with current SA legislation and both local and international best practices.

Mr Sipho Moela, MCom (Industrial and Organisational Psychology), Department of Higher Education and Training, South Africa

This is an ***EAP roadmap*** for management, EAP practitioners and students who aspire to become EAP practitioners.

For management, it provides practical solutions to the traditional organisational challenges that impact on efficiency, productivity and service delivery due to low staff morale, absenteeism, substance abuse, employee health and wellness, and the needs of troubled employees.

For the EAP practitioner, it offers guidance on how to establish and operate an effective EAP programme within the workplace that considers stakeholder involvement as being critical, costing implications, and the implementation of interventions that would benefit organisations. Furthermore, it professionalises the EAP practice by introducing various theories, interventions, approaches and methods of delivering EAP services.

Finally, this book equips and prepares aspirant **EAP students** with knowledge and insight into the dynamics of organisational health and wellness and helps them to understand the application of behavioural science interventions within the context of addressing the needs of troubled employees and forging stakeholder relations with management and organised labour.

Matsie Litheko, MA (Social Work Management), Chief Director: Human Resources Policy and Strategy Department of Justice and Constitutional Development

A healthy workforce is the foundation of organisational success. No organisation, small or large, can survive without energised and healthy employees who believe in the organisation's mission and how to achieve it. This book is loaded with theory ***and*** practical applications and is an ideal handbook for both academics and practitioners in the field.

Prof Yvonne Joubert, Department of Human Resource Management, University of South Africa

This book unlocks the key competencies required for EAP specialists to operate successfully in organisations today. *Employee Assistance Programmes* examines the new role of EAP specialists and how they can to add business value through workplace performance.

Siphokazi Bokwe, MCom (HRM), General Manager: Learning and Development/ Performance Management, SANParks

Employee Assistance Programmes will show you how to attract and retain talented employees, as well as equip and support leaders with the ability to harness the talents and abilities of their staff. This is an essential guidebook to help build the capacity of EAP practitioners to enhance the performance and efficiency of organisations in attracting and retaining critical competencies.

Bruce Ndumiso Tashe, BCom, BTh, MBA, Laetoli (Pty) Ltd

Having served for more than 20 years as a psychologist in the SA Police Service, I witnessed the establishment of an in-house EAP from the mid-90s. This was associated with several misunderstandings of the role of the EAP practitioner, which consisted of a multi-disciplinary team, including the various categories of psychologists, psychometrists, counsellors, social workers as well as spiritual workers or chaplains. This not only led to conflict between the different occupations, but it also contributed to serious misconceptions of the EAP by the clients as well as the management of the organisation.

This book is structured and presented in such a way that will assist *existing* EAP practitioners, as well as practitioners in training, to find and perform their specific roles and responsibilities within the broader EAP, especially in terms of a multi-disciplinary team. Given my practical experience, I would strongly recommend this book to anyone involved with an EAP.

Professor Anton Grobler, Leadership and Organisational Behaviour, Editor: South African Journal of Labour Relations (SAJLR), Graduate School of Business Leadership (SBL)

This book reminds readers of the potential of EAPs and the role they play in improving employee performance. The overall discussion, analysis and presentation of the content makes this book interesting and adaptable to the South African working environment, therefore it is beneficial to both academics and practitioners in the field.

Dr Michelle Fontainha de Sousa Sabbagha, Industrial and Organisational Psychologist, Senior Manager: FX e-commerce Client Services, Global Markets and Corporate Investment Banking

First published in 2018.

ISBN: 978-1-86922-737-1
eISBN: 978-1-86922-738-8 (ePDF)

Published by KR Publishing
P O Box 3954
Randburg
2125
Republic of South Africa

Tel: (011) 706-6009
Fax: (011) 706-1127
E-mail: orders@knowres.co.za
Website: www.kr.co.za

Printed and bound: HartWood Digital Printing, 243 Alexandra Avenue, Halfway House, Midrand
Typesetting, layout and design: Cia Joubert, cia@knowres.co.za
Cover design: Marlene de'Lorme, marlene@knowres.co.za
Editing & proofreading: Jennifer Renton, jenniferrenton@live.co.za
Project management: Cia Joubert, cia@knowres.co.za
Index created with TExtract / www.Texyz.com

EMPLOYEE ASSISTANCE PROGRAMMES

Theory and practical applications

By

Prof Ophillia Ledimo
Prof Nico Martins

2018

ACKNOWLEDGEMENTS

We would like to thank our publishers for their support and encouragement. We would also like to thank our clients and students over the years, from whom we have learnt so much, and whose inputs have helped to shape our understanding of EAP and the format of the book.

The authors

TABLE OF CONTENTS

LIST OF TABLES

LIST OF FIGURES

ABOUT THE AUTHORS

Prof Ophillia Ledimo

Ophillia is registered with the Health Professions Council of South Africa as an Industrial Psychologist and a registered Social Worker. She holds a Doctorate in Industrial and Organisational Psychology and is Full Professor and Chair of the Department of IOP at the University of South Africa (Unisa). She has also led the Research Ethics Committee for the Department of IOP and has supervised Masters and Doctoral students to the completion of their degrees. Ophillia has published articles and presented papers at international and national academic forums, and was presented with a Research Award by the College of Economic and Management Sciences at Unisa. Prior to joining Unisa, Ophillia worked for FORD in the Human Resource Department managing their Employee Assistance Programme. She also worked for the Brunnel Institute of Social Sciences of South Africa (BIOSSA) as an Organisational Development Consultant. At BIOSSA, she was responsible for training, organisational development programmes and assessment/development centres. Ophillia has consulting experience in the field of organisational development and psychological assessments within the public and private sectors. Her e-mail is manetom@unisa.ac.za.

Prof Nico Martins

Nico holds a PhD in Industrial Psychology and is registered at the Health Professions Council of SA (HPCSA) as a psychologist and as a chartered HR practitioner at the SA Board for People Practices (SABPP). Over and above his own research, a number of Nico's Masters and Doctoral students have conducted further research into organisational culture, focusing on the assessment of sub-cultures; the relationship between organisational culture and concepts such as organisational commitment, employee satisfaction, perceived leader emotional competency, personality type, and occupational health; and employee engagement. This collaborative research has led to the validation of assessment tools in organisational culture, organisational climate, organisational trust, employee engagement and employment equity.

Nico has attended several specialised programmes at the National Training Laboratories (NTL) in the USA, and is an international affiliate of the Society of Industrial and Organisational Psychology (SIOP) in the USA.

Nico is currently a Research Professor at the Department of Industrial and Organisational Psychology at the University of South Africa (Unisa), where he specialises in the field of organisational psychology. His fields of expertise are organisational development and change. Nico has published over 100 refereed conference papers and academic articles both locally and internationally. He is acknowledged by the National Research Foundation (NRF) as a seasonal researcher, and has presented papers at more than 50 national and international conferences based on work conducted with various local and global companies.

Together with Ellen Martins, Nico founded Organisational Diagnostics CC more than 20 years ago. They have since participated in more than 500 qualitative and quantitative organisational survey projects and have surveyed various Southern African and international organisations. A number of Nico's Masters and Doctoral students have further researched the mentioned constructs. He has extensive knowledge in the fields of organisational assessments and interventions, and is the co-editor and author of several books and chapters in his field of expertise.

PREFACE

The current business environment requires South African organisations to focus on performance and efficiency. For this reason, there is a need for them to manage their Employee Assistance Programmes (EAPs) in a way that will result in the retention of talented employees, improved performance and positive employer-employee relationships. To assist organisations to increase performance and efficiency, it is important to build the capacity of EAP managers, coordinators and practitioners.

This capacity building should focus on the following critical competencies required for proficiency:

- The ability to conduct EAP needs analyses and assessments in order to describe the services required by the organisation to deal with employee- and work-related dysfunctions.
- The ability to initiate and implement EAPs in a credible and ethical manner through appropriate stakeholder engagement, marketing and the ethical conduct of service providers.
- The ability to develop a policy and procedures that are specific to an organisation, in order to have a framework in place to guide the successful implementation of EAPs in the workplace.
- The ability to conduct impact assessments in order to assist organisations with the evaluation, monitoring and continuous improvement of EAPs based on their quality assurance standards.

The lack of guidance on these competencies provided the impetus for this book, which serves as a manual for EAP practice. Given the importance of EAP, it is interesting to note the lack of guidance in the form of textbooks on this topic. As the authors, we hope that this book will assist organisations to focus on employee wellness and performance enhancement in their organisations. We further hope that the clarification of concepts, roles, functions, principles and practical examples will assist in the successful implementation and monitoring of EAPs.

Broadly speaking, readers will come to understand how to formulate guidelines or processes for the successful execution of an EAP in their organisation, to develop policies, and to influence assessment measures that promote the ethical and credible provision of EAPs in the workplace.

This book consists of 12 chapters, which cover most of the core concepts of EAPs. Given the background of the authors, an industrial psychological approach was followed when writing the chapters. The book was written as an integrated EAP process. What follows is an overview of these. Chapters 1 - 6 was written by Prof Ledimo and chapters 7 - 12 by Prof Martins.

Chapter 1: The nature and value of EAPs

The purpose of this chapter is to describe the historical development of EAPs, which will provide you, as a practitioner or manager, insight into the existence of EAPs in the international and South African contexts. Secondly, the role and function of enhancing work adjustment at an individual, group, and organisational level is discussed. It is expected that this chapter will help you to develop an understanding of EAPs as a concept in a multi-faceted professional field.

Chapter 2: EAP needs analysis and scope of practice

As an essential aspect of EAP is to conduct an initial needs assessment, one focus of this chapter is on the different types of diagnostic tools and processes that can be used across the various levels of an organisation. Secondly, the principles and scope of EAPs are explored as proactive and reactive systems to manage the work dysfunctions of employees and groups. This chapter also describes the importance and benefits of conducting a needs analysis for an EAP. A discussion of the data collection and analysis process using qualitative and quantitative methods is presented to allow the reader to choose the most relevant methods for their organisation. The value of feedback to share the findings in a report or feedback sessions is also discussed.

Chapter 3: Initiation of an EAP

The initiation of EAPs in organisations is based on the theoretical model adopted to deal with work dysfunctions and maladjustment. This chapter guides practitioners in the field to focus on reactive and proactive approaches. Service delivery models that can be initiated can be internal (in-house), external (outsourced) or comprehensive in nature. The chapter concludes by discussing resource allocation, focusing on the comprehensive identification, allocation and management of the required human and financial resources for a successful EAP implementation.

Chapter 4: Implementation of an EAP at the individual, group and organisational levels

In this chapter, the focus is on the various ways in which dysfunctions or maladjustments at an individual, group or organisational level can be addressed. The scope and context of this chapter focuses on different EAP interventions, namely counselling, coaching, group work, workshops and life skills development. These interventions are applicable across all levels and are used to enhance and address performance issues in the workplace. The advantages and disadvantages of counselling, therapy, trauma debriefing, crisis management, group work and life skills development are discussed to enable a practitioner to make informed decisions in practice.

Chapter 5: Stakeholder management and marketing of an EAP

Knowing the relevant key stakeholders in an organisation can enable an EAP manager or practitioner to gain their support for the initiation and implementation of an EAP. A marketing plan and strategy is essential to create awareness and increase the utilisation of an EAP, which is why this chapter describes the process of identifying all internal and external stakeholders to engage within the organisation. Lastly, the author provides practitioners or managers with guidelines they can follow in the process of formulating an internal marketing plan on EAP services for all employees.

Chapter 6: Ethical considerations for implementing an EAP

Knowledge and management of ethical considerations is crucial for the credible implementation of an EAP in an organisation. The scope and context of this chapter focuses on how practitioners or managers can comply with the relevant professional ethics in the provision of EAP services to protect the rights of employees as users. The ability to determine ethical dilemmas and to deal with them is of critical importance for the successful practice of an EAP.

Chapter 7: Development of an EAP policy and procedures

The existence of an EAP policy is important in organisations because of the ongoing developments in this field. EAPs were first created in the 1940s with a focus on the use and abuse of alcohol in terms of job performance. Over time, the emphasis broadened to include other personal issues that may influence job performance. This chapter focuses on the use and participation of employees in EAPs, and also highlights the policy of voluntary participation in the process. This implies that employees and their next of kin are guided by the policy to make an informed decision to use or participate in EAPs. In describing the components that should be covered in an EAP policy, the chapter indicates the procedures and types of services offered in such a programme. Lastly, the role of the employees in balancing work and personal life demands is also discussed.

Chapter 8: Procedure for EAP services

This chapter presents a myriad of EAP services offered by practitioners in their organisations. The chapter further highlights the responsibility of HR departments to determine the services and processes of EAP service delivery, which should be included in the policy document. Furthermore, the services, which should be supported by the organisation's capacity to provide human and financial resources, are explored. Reference is also made in this chapter to research in the field in some South African organisations pertaining to the discussed aspects.

Chapter 9: Role, function and ethical principles of a professional team

EAP professionals are guided by the Employee Assistance Ethics Professionals Association (EAPA) Code of Ethics, which provides guidance about how they should conduct themselves. The code clearly defines the acceptable standards of behaviour for the benefit of the client (employees, employers, unions, colleagues, other professionals, community and society). If organisations process any personal information of their employees then the Protection of Personal Information Act (2013) applies. These prescripts and legislation are all discussed in this chapter.

Chapter 10: Quality management of EAPs

Adherence to professional standards and guidelines ensures viable EAPs. The purpose of the non-regulatory guidelines is to assist all relevant stakeholders to establish quality EAPs in accordance with international best practices and to enhance existing EAPs.[1] In chapter 10, the functions of an EAP quality assurance committee, quality assurance measures and standards for the practitioner and manager are discussed.

Chapter 11: EAP impact assessment

Chapter 11 outlines the importance of an EAP assessment and a process that can be followed to create and perform an assessment. This chapter should enable readers to determine which tools are relevant for impact assessments in order to identify gaps with regard to EAP implementation in their organisations. A continuous improvement plan is also presented which can be used to address the gaps or limitations of a programme. The chapter focuses on the value of impact assessments of EAPs, the evaluation strategies of EAP services at an individual, group and organisational level, and EAP evaluation and monitoring tools. The monitoring tools highlight the use of focus groups, interviews and satisfaction surveys to evaluate an EAP programme.

Chapter 12: Report writing and continuous improvement for all levels

Report writing is important in the process of keeping a record of the services provided to EAP recipients in an organisation. This chapter provides insight into the compilation of individual and group EAP reports, the best practices for EAP, and the various principles, tools and processes that can be applied for the continuous improvement of EAP initiatives in the workplace. Lastly, the role of the EAP manager in implementing continuous improvement plans is discussed.

Chapter 1

NATURE AND VALUE OF AN EAP

INTRODUCTION

Employee Assistance Programmes (EAPs) are growing in attractiveness to organisations in the public and private sectors, due to the number of employees who exhibit poor performance, high absenteeism and tardiness, as well as the number of those who are affected by HIV/Aids, violence, as well as alcohol and drug abuse. The focus of this chapter is largely on describing the concept of an EAP; any practitioner or manager in this field is expected to have a comprehensive understanding of the historical development of the construct of an EAP, its dimensions and its value in the current world of work.

WHAT IS AN EAP?

The purpose of an EAP is tertiary prevention, or identifying and treating, curing or managing existing problems such as substance abuse, psychological and physical illness, and other personal problems which affect employees' work performance and organisational productivity.

Jacobson[2] confirmed that EAP professionals provide the majority of mental health services to adults in the workplace. The idea behind these services is to improve troubled employees' chances of recuperating and remaining employed. The programmes used are typically job-based, with employers providing troubled employees with the necessary counselling and other services/facilities to overcome their problems. Rajin[3] argued that EAPs are not unique to South Africa, but noted that the circumstances under which they are implemented in each organisation are one of a kind.

Modern EAPs provide employees with multiple internal and external services, covering many of the issues and problems that arise in their personal and work lives. From a curative and preventative perspective, EAPs typically offer various treatment programmes, for instance for combating substance abuse, or recovering from injuries/illnesses as a result of pollution or contact with toxic substances. Other activities pertain to programme policies and procedures, negotiation procedures and grievance handling, education on and training in the use of the EAPs, and supervisory consultation.

Currently, EAPs offer probably the best example of comprehensive health promotion programmes in the workplace. As part of employee wellbeing initiatives, the aim is to provide staff (and even their relatives and management) with multiple health and counselling services, to assist them with dealing more effectively with personal, social and work-related problems. EAPs may include very specific health-related services and facilities both in and outside of organisations, in addition to offering macro-services which deal with employees in the context of their external environments and broader community programmes.

It is obvious that effective work-site health promotion involves not only employee health, but also that of the organisation and society at large. It is therefore essential that all parties be involved in the planning, design, implementation and maintenance of related initiatives. Most organisations provide health promotion services, either internally or in conjunction with other companies or external providers, to grant more employees access to diverse facilities. As comprehensive health-promotion offerings, EAPs are quite diversified and may mean different things to different people. Such differences may be evident in the multitude of services on offer, and in the wide array of professionals/clients involved in EAPs. Some functions in organisations, such as specific training programmes, may be related to certain health-promoting services which EAPs provide. In fact, all functions in organisations should contribute to the optimal psychological adjustment of employees and their health in general.

The literature describes EAPs as follows:

- Taylor, Holosko, Wayne-Smith and Feit[4] defined EAPs as employment-based services whose purpose is to assist those individuals experiencing personal problems, by both assessing the nature of their difficulties and making referrals to appropriate helping resources.
- Du Plessis[5] argued that EAPs are aimed at linking employees with personal problems to appropriate resources, in order to correct or prevent deterioration in job performance.
- Sonnenstuhl and Trice[6] defined EAPs as job-based programmes operating within organisations "for the purpose of identifying troubled employees, motivating them to resolve their troubles, and providing access to counselling or treatment for those who need the services".
- Berridge[7] indicated that EAPs in the United States (US) function as an effective bureaucracy to deliver conformist promptings to employees who transgress the tenets of good behaviour.
- Alker and McHugh[8] noted that the UK Employee Assistance Professionals Association defines EAP as "a mechanism for making counselling and other forms of assistance available to a designated workforce on a systematic and uniform basis, and to recognized standards".
- Robbins and DeCenzo[9] stated that EAPs are programmes offered by organisations to help employees overcome personal and health-related problems.

- The Employee Assistance Professional Association – South Africa[10] described EAPs as involving the identification and resolution of "productivity problems associated with employees impaired by personal concerns".
- Rajin[11] defined EAPs as workplace-based programmes, offered free of charge, as support interventions for distressed employees.
- The International Employee Assistance Professionals Association[12] indicated that EAPs, by definition, help employers address productivity issues on two levels: they advise the leadership of work organisations and help "employee clients" identify and resolve a broad range of personal concerns, including occupational stress that may affect job performance.

The above definitions suggest that EAPs can be described as worksite-based programmes and/or resources designed to benefit both employers and employees. This implies that EAPs help businesses and organisations to address productivity and performance-related issues, by helping employees to identify and resolve any personal concerns that might affect their productivity or performance.

THE HISTORICAL DEVELOPMENT OF EAPs IN SOUTH AFRICA AND INTERNATIONALLY

International history of the development of EAPs

The establishment of EAPs began in America. The 1940s and 1950s were a milestone in the history of these interventions, when occupational alcoholism programmes were introduced to provide assistance to employees struggling with drinking problems.[13] The EAPs assisted employers with the alcohol-related difficulties that their employees faced on a continuous basis, such as absenteeism and decreased levels of job performance.[14] However, the earliest programmes, which were non-psychiatric, had already been developed in the mid-1920s, and were supervised by a group of counsellors together with other plant employees. Because the counsellors had received no clinical training, they were only allowed to make use of interviews. Making diagnoses, issuing prescriptions and giving advice were therefore avoided.[15] In 1944, the National Council on Alcoholism was formed to educate companies on the merits of alcoholism programmes.

In the 1980s, EAPs, which continued to maintain their focus on alcoholism and drug abuse counselling, broadened their scope to include issues related to job stress. John Hall established an Employee Assistance Programme in the United Kingdom in 1983, in his role as personnel manager for the US-owned Control Data Corporation.[16] These programmes have since gained significant recognition on matters relating to employee mental healthcare in the USA and Europe.[17] They are more popular in Western countries and are somewhat rare in territories in Asia, Latin America, Africa and the former Soviet Union. Given the spread of globalisation, however, EAPs are starting to evolve and are being made available in countries that previously mainly offered government-sponsored health and welfare services.

For Berridge and Cooper,[18] EAPs are programmatic interventions at the workplace – usually at the level of the individual employee – which use behavioural science knowledge and methods. The purpose is to control certain work-related problems (notably alcoholism, drug abuse and mental health problems) that adversely affect job performance, with the objective of enabling the individual to return to making a full contribution and to attaining full functioning in his/her personal life.

Since 2000, autonomous EAP associations (separate from those based in the USA) have emerged in Europe, Asia, Central and South America, to help individuals manage dysfunctional stressors.[19] These programmes have also received attention in Japan, where they are used to alleviate depression and counteract suicidal behaviours, while promoting the mental health of employees.[20] A study of 142 EAPs from across Canada revealed a vibrant range of programming where the focus remained on the individual, and noted that a significant minority of EAPs had branched out and were offering services to enhance organisational wellness.[21]

The latest development in EAPs involves a shift from offering counselling towards providing treatment to alcoholic employees.[22] These interventions are therefore defined as employee-based programmes aimed at identifying, motivating, counselling and providing treatment to troubled staff.[23] The programmes are thus key instruments in addressing any internal, external, as well as social problems affecting employee wellbeing.[24] Not only do the programmes deal with employees' personal matters, but also with issues related to their emotions (such as marital strife, physical illness, stress and depression). These programmes, which are designed to enhance employee performance, are known for their positive effect on job satisfaction and productivity. They are preventive measures modelled on alcoholism assessment and referral centres in the USA.[25]

While the field of EAP is growing internationally, a comprehensive body of research appears to be lacking when it comes to supporting how and why EAPs can be used, or providing best practice guidelines for service delivery. Joseph and Walker[26] stated that, specifically in the Australian context, many assumptions and claims relating to EAPs dominate what little research actually exists. Internationally, the effective use of EAPs is regarded as enabling both management and the employee or staff cohort to assist employees and their families with behavioural problems such as alcoholism and substance abuse.[27] These programmes offer beneficial services, which are financed by the organisation, to resolve any personal and/or family matters affecting employees, that may be impeding their productivity.[28] Employee participation is, however, voluntary, or is done through medical referrals or referrals by supervisors or peers. One of several areas of contention within the EAP field is the conflict between management prerogatives and labour rights with respect to the work environment – the EAP performs a crucial function in mediating between the interests of these two parties.[29]

South African history of the development of EAPs

In South Africa, the first EAP was established in 1986 by the Chamber of Mines. According to the Employee Assistance Professionals Association of South Africa (EAPA-SA), EAPs are regarded as resources aimed at enhancing employee and workplace effectiveness through the prevention, identification and resolution of personal and productivity issues.[30] A study by Gerber[31] found that EAPs were initiated in the private sector in the 1980s, with a focus on alcoholism and substance abuse. In her research, Bell[32] found that EAPs are a relatively new service offering within government departments, with a proposal for their introduction only submitted in February 2001 to the Department of Water Affairs and Forestry of the Northern Province. According to Ndhlovu,[33] the concept of EAPs was introduced in most South African government departments by the early 2000s alongside the HIV/Aids Action Project, which was aimed at minimising the impact of the disease in the workplace, both in government departments and across South Africa as a whole.

The utilisation of EAPs in some organisations is low due to the social stigma associated with visiting counsellors or psychiatrists. Bophela[34] emphasised that EAPs should be outsourced and designed to reflect on specific matters in order to provide organisations with a competitive advantage, ensure maximum efficiency and encourage low absenteeism.

In South Africa, as in other countries, EAPs are not governed by specific laws, except that the services offered through such programmes must comply with human rights and labour laws. On a functional level, the Employee Assistance Society of South Africa (EASSA) is an interest group which, together with universities and the Institute of Personnel Management (IPM), manages the interests, examination and registration of EAP consultants. A National Employee Assistance Programme Committee, on which many employers in South Africa are represented, meets at regular intervals and also organises annual conferences.

At a legislative level, occupational health services (including psychological health services) are influenced by a country's policies and practices.[35] In South Africa it is possible to distinguish between the period prior to 1994, during which policies and practices were determined by a white-dominated socioeconomic and political dispensation, and the period post-1994 to date, in which transformation has been characterised by a political system.

Since 1994, under various initiatives – especially the Reconstruction and Development Programme (RDP) – various steps have been taken to transform and restructure all health services, including occupational health, where the emphasis is on upholding human rights in a healthy and safe working environment.[36] Following the large-scale migration of workers from rural to urban areas due to the development of a large mining industry and various commissions investigating occupational diseases and concomitant labour issues, legislation regulating labour practices was passed as early as 1911, and since then more Acts have followed.

The first real legislation on occupational health which aimed to control conditions in industry was the Factories, Machinery and Building Act, 22 of 1941 (RSA, 1941), which was later changed to the Occupational Health and Safety Act, 85 of 1993 (RSA, 1993b). In general, health matters are regulated by various pieces of legislation and associated bodies which control the application thereof. An important government agency is the Department of Health, which regulates health matters through the Health Act, 63 of 1977 (RSA, 1977), and as amended (see National Health Act, 61 of 2003), and specific provisions in other Acts which are applied by various other institutions. Examples of specific Acts are the Mine Health and Safety Act, 29 of 1996 (RSA, 1996), the Nursing Amendment Act, 5 of 1995 (RSA, 1995), and the Mental Health Act, 18 of 1973 (RSA, 1973).

Various statutory bodies function under legislation, such as the Health Professions Council of South Africa, the National Air Pollution Advisory Committee and the South African Nursing Council, while institutions like the Medical Bureau for Occupational Diseases (MBOD) and the National Centre for Occupational Health (NCOD) study and monitor diverse aspects of occupational health. In addition to the Department of Health, various government agencies and their statutory bodies and related structures regulate industry and labour practices.

The Department of Labour regulates important legislation which may have an impact on occupational health, such as the Occupational Health and Safety Act, 85 of 1993 (RSA, 1993b), the Compensation for Occupational Injuries and Diseases Act, 130 of 1993 (RSA, 1993a), the Labour Relations Act, 66 of 1995 (RSA, 1995) and the Basic Conditions of Employment Act, 104 of 1992 (RSA, 1992). Structures which assist the Department of Labour are the Workmen's Compensation Commissioner, the Industrial Courts, and the National Manpower and Training Boards. Private initiatives like the National Occupational Safety Association (NOSA) are tasked with training and promoting health and safety at work, either on a permanent or a contractual basis, in many companies in South Africa. Although most of the legislation and controls concern physical health and safety as well as related illnesses and hygiene factors, they also pertain indirectly (and often directly) to psychological health, given the close association between physical and psychological health or illness and adjustment or maladjustment.

Serious physical injuries sustained during workplace accidents, or injuries and illness as a result of pollution, may have serious psychological consequences for many employees. The purpose of the aforementioned controls is to ensure the healthiest and best fit between people and their physical work environments, especially with regard to work design, work equipment, physical working conditions (free from pollution and noise, and with adequate illumination and ventilation) and work schedules.

Other labour issues that are controlled are more directly related to the subjective experience of work, such as minimum benefits and services, labour relations, the training and development of employees, and other matters relating to employee and employer rights and responsibilities. An important aspect which relates to basic human rights in the workplace concerns the stipulations in the labour laws that all human resource management functions shall be fair and non-discriminatory. These stipulations include, for example, policies and practices for assessing employees, decisions and interventions based on such assessments, or other interventions which may influence individual employees and their career and health status. It is believed that in the South African work context, many organisations apply regulations to health and safety quite accurately and stringently, but many still do not, thus employee health may be a neglected phenomenon.

In this country, large corporations and government departments commonly implement EAPs, however their rapid growth has been reactive, with few programmes focusing on proactive interventions. In many instances their utilisation and management practices are still in the process of evolving.

EAPs AS A MULTI-PROFESSIONAL FIELD

EAPs involve various professions, just as EAP professionals represent various disciplines. While their professional training might vary, they all work with employees, and often employees' family members, to support them with personal problems that have the potential to affect the workplace.[37] Such programmes are not limited to one specific profession, hence their effective implementation may require the services of, amongst others, medical practitioners; nursing professionals; social workers; and clinical, counselling, industrial and organisational psychologists. In some organisations the human resource team of the EAP might include dentists, pharmacists and physiotherapists. Being a multi-disciplinary offering, different professionals who are involved in an EAP programme provide their services to employees and organisations, as per their professional scope of practice.

As professionals, industrial and organisational psychologists are critical to the services offered by EAPs. According to Bergh and Theron,[38] Industrial and Organisational Psychology (IOP) is a branch of psychology that utilises psychological knowledge in the work context to assess, develop and influence individual employees and groups, as well as related organisational processes. As an applied field of psychology, IOP focuses on human behaviour in the workplace and has become a professional practice in its own right.[39] Since the main objective of this profession is to provide interventions that enhance individuals' quality of work-life and work performance, in addition to improving organisational health, EAPs are a strong focus area of this profession.

As indicated above, clinical, counselling, industrial and organisational psychologists are mostly appointed with the responsibility of taking part in the implementation of EAPs in their organisations. These different types of psychologists fulfil different roles in the field of EAP, based on their scope of practice. Their tasks may include:

- conducting assessments using psychological tests and psychometrics;
- formulating diagnoses based on their assessments;
- providing interventions at the individual, group and organisational levels;
- conducting programme impact assessments or evaluations; and
- presenting prognoses for employees' situations.

EAPs similarly form part of the social work profession, where the social work role can be described as occupational social work – a specialised field of practice where the focus is on the individual employee. Occupational social work provides specific social services under a contractual agreement, in terms of which professionally trained social workers or institutions (such as voluntary or social agencies) can be called on to provide the necessary services to the employees of trade unions or work organisations.[40] Such programmes and services fall under the auspices of labour or management, utilising professional social workers to serve employees and the legitimate social welfare needs of a labour or industrial organisation.

The following are elements which form part of the tasks of those occupational social workers who manage EAPs:

- They use select social work methods and skills (e.g. casework and counselling).
- They create a model of workplace programme practices (e.g. an EAP).
- The focus of their service is on employees with social welfare needs, and under whose auspices those services are delivered (labour, management or joint).
- They consult on individual employee needs and policy situations.
- They offer client assessments and interventions, using short-term and crisis intervention methodologies.
- They facilitate negotiations and the resolution of conflict between employees and their supervisors/managers.

- They advocate on behalf of clients and make referrals to or develop relationships with community-based service agencies (adapted from Mogorosi).[41]

THE DIFFERENT DIMENSIONS OF AN EAP

It is clear that EAPs in organisations are multi-dimensional. At the core, it is possible to differentiate between the psychological, occupational health, human resources and social dimensions.

Psychological dimension

The state of an employee's mental health has an influence on his/her work behaviour. The psychological dimension of EAPs involves practitioners ensuring that employees receive the necessary professional help to deal with any mental illnesses or abnormal behaviours they might exhibit. Therefore, introducing programmes aimed at alleviating stress-related problems is essential, as these help to reduce sickness, absenteeism, employee turnover and workplace accidents. The most common of these programmes educate employees about the nature of stress, encourage them to change certain patterns of behaviour, and provide stress management interventions such as progressive muscle relaxation, cognitive restructuring and meditation.[42]

EAPs that deal with stress are aimed at empowering employees to cope with personal problems, so that they can focus more on their jobs and be more productive. These aspects need to be prioritised in modern organisations. EAPs thus play an essential role in supporting employees as they address stressors related to health, alcohol or drug abuse, and problems related to family, finances, legal matters, marriage and any other personal issues. The aim is to help employees improve their mental and emotional health, which will lead them to make better choices when it comes to their physical health and reduce the risk of illnesses developing into costly and more damaging chronic conditions.

Very few individuals who are in need of substance abuse treatment actually receive it. One of the most commonly cited barriers to receiving treatment for substance abuse is the time treatment seekers wait to enter a treatment or rehab facility. By providing easy access through EAPs, organisations are able to eliminate these time barriers and subsequently help employees improve their behavioural wellbeing.[43] It is through continuous communication and reflection on the effective existence of such EAPs within organisations that employee performance, productivity and work attendance can be improved. EAPs are grounded in a humanistic paradigm that encourages organisations to meet the needs of troubled employees.[44] These include services such as the management of work and life stress, substance abuse, and work–family conflict-related issues.

Occupational health dimension

This dimension focuses on any medical conditions affecting employee wellness. The management of work injuries, chronic diseases and pandemics amongst employees has been the focus area of EAPs in organisations for some time now. Counselling plays an important role in mitigating the spread and management of HIV/Aids, as it is through counselling that individuals and their families can be helped to control and manage the spread of the disease.[45] EAP counsellors who focus on HIV/Aids have an obligation to facilitate behavioural change, promote the early management of opportunistic and sexually transmitted infections, facilitate referrals for social and peer support, and normalise HIV/Aids and its stigma.

In organisations, the introduction of counselling programmes for people living with HIV/Aids has made innovative, cost-effective and patient-friendly approaches available to employees.[46] Such programmes are important in providing prevention and service strategies for both men and women.[47] Because these programmes are a national priority, they should be aligned with national strategic plans. This implies that organisational policies and procedures should address the rights of those infected with and affected by HIV/Aids, and ensure that confidentiality surrounding such issues remains a priority.

Human resources dimension

Bophela[48] posited that workplace dysfunctions that require EAPs are aggravated by factors such as extended working hours, toxic work environments, difficulties in relationships between co-workers and management, bullying and harassment from management. Physical working conditions such as office temperature, humidity, ventilation, illumination and noise can affect employees' wellbeing, and ultimately their performance. These conditions have a significant impact on employees' work behaviours, as they influence productivity, the quality of their output, and accidents, which, in extreme cases, can result in compromised health (e.g. cardiovascular disease) or even death. As it is the main focus of the human resource dimension to create ideal working conditions and relationships for all employees, this requires compliance with any and all legislation relating to office or factory environments.

Social dimension

At a social level, EAPs are concerned with the wellbeing of employees within the context of their families, communities and societies, hence programmes for family support are offered to provide services to employees and their family members, while ensuring that employee performance is not affected negatively.[49] These programmes can assist employees with finding a work-life balance, by accommodating flexible work schedules which allow them to manage multiple responsibilities.

The management team is therefore responsible for ensuring that these programmes provide employees with coping strategies. The abovementioned dimensions are common in organisations that are committed to perfecting the competitive skills of their employees. Organisations which institute their EAP initiatives based on these dimensions tend to achieve high levels of work commitment, employee satisfaction and engagement, and low levels of absenteeism. These dimensions not only improve the work-life of employees, but also act as building blocks for those organisations that value customer satisfaction and service delivery.

EAPs IN THE WORLD OF WORK

Since the 1980s, South African companies have recognised the potential of EAPs and the role they play in enhancing employee performance through improving staff members' physical and mental health, as well as improving their life-management knowledge and skills. In the world of work, organisations that have implemented EAP programmes continue to reap rewards for themselves and their employees. Many South African companies do not, however, perceive these programmes as essential instruments of human resource management when it comes to managing the impact of Aids, violence, substance abuse and transformation. Their employee support programmes mainly focus on physical disease management; combating high cholesterol and high blood pressure; giving nutritional advice; and promoting the benefits of exercise, quitting smoking and weight management. Nonetheless, the current South African government recognises the importance of addressing issues related to mental health, substance abuse, and Aids in the workplace. Government institutions such as the South African Police Service (SAPS) have, for instance, institutionalised EAS (employee assistance services) in order to provide specific assistance and support to their most valuable assets – their human resources.[50]

EAPs thus encourage the maintenance of a workforce that contributes optimally and is sufficiently healthy in both body and mind. In companies, EAPs assist in managing the "issues of the day", which can include change, affirmative action, transformation, restructuring, training and development, downsizing and violence prevention. By providing workshops and consultation services, the focus falls equally on the employee and the organisation as a client.

Globally, EAPs play such a significant role that they are positioned at the core of the business structure. In South Africa, however, they appear to be have very little influence on decision makers, when compared to first-world countries such as the USA and the United Kingdom (UK).[51] Nonetheless, EAPs have become part of the landscape and are expected to be available to meet a need, as and when it arises. Csiernik and Csiernik[52] indicated that EAPs provide helping resources (both peer-related and professional) that many would otherwise not be able to access, or not access as readily.

The following emerging models have gained prominence in the world of work:[53]

- EAP are utilising distance counselling through call-centres rather than face-to-face interventions. Sessions are conducted telephonically and via e-counselling systems.
- Ancient thinking and interventions are finding their way back into EAPs, including art therapy and creativity-based interventions.
- The traditionally reactive style of EAP models has been replaced by resilient, proactive interventions.
- EAPs play a major role in improving employee productivity, raising morale, fostering a work ethic and helping employees deal with bereavement through spirituality and faith/interfaith programmes.
- Embedded/free EAPs have emerged as an EAP industry.
- EAPs are assisting organisations to manage diversity/generational differences in the workplace.
- EAPs help organisations understand and address the impact that engagement has on employee productivity.

ROLES AND FUNCTIONS OF EAPs

The reasons for establishing EAPs span an entire benevolence spectrum; there are probably as many reasons for establishing such programmes as there are organisations wishing to introduce some kind of workplace-based service for their employees.

Some EAPs are implemented with positive motives (others with negative motives!), and some without management having any knowledge of the subject, despite having programmes in place. The majority of organisations establish programmes for practical reasons, including the expectation that such interventions will produce the intended results, whatever those may be.

The following section focuses on the functions and roles of EAPs at the individual, team/group and organisational levels.

Individual level

Any individual can be described in terms of various systems (biological, social, marriage, family, kinship, religion and culture, etc.). An employee's potential for the organisation lies in the qualities (capabilities, knowledge, skills) s/he brings to the workplace. His/her self-image, occupational concepts, interpersonal skills, behaviour, communication styles, illnesses and psychological problems were formed (and are being formed) through a process of continuous interaction with the environment, which includes cultural and other influences.

Employers are increasingly requesting EAPs that can provide support services to employees following traumatic events such as workplace violence or natural disasters.[54] The success of an individual's work role and his/her intrapersonal and interpersonal relationships may largely be a function of his/her interaction in the organisation. Since employees are the organisation's most valuable asset, their wellbeing plays an important role in making the organisation productive and competitive. Joseph and Walker[55] stated that by offering EAPs as a support service to staff, organisations may be seen to meet the terms of employees' psychological contracts, by positively contributing to staff wellbeing. EAPs are therefore important in proving that management adopts a proactive stance to the health and wellness of employees. The leadership of an organisation can ensure employees' health by providing wellness knowledge to empower and assist them in sustaining a healthy lifestyle.[56] At an individual level, EAPs can help employees to manage the balance between work and non-work demands. The role of the EAP professional is to identify behavioural, social and health problems that may affect employees' performance, and to decrease their stress levels insofar as these affect organisational performance.

EAPs benefit individual employees' performance, as they recognise both their work and their dignity.[57] These services help to enhance productivity and the social functioning of employees[58] by reconciling employees' personal and work lives. The role and function of EAP practitioners is to move away from a 'one-size-fits-all' offering, by allowing individual employees to find a tailor-made work-life balance.

Although such programmes encourage managers to translate family-friendly work policies into practice, the level of perceived support that employees receive from their direct line managers depends on each manager's personal beliefs around, and his/her attitude towards, EAPs.[59]

Another concern regarding the primary focus of EAPs, as raised in a Canadian study, is that they are designed to assist individuals in need to use the programmes voluntarily, in attempts to cope with personal problems.[60] Employees might, of their own accord, seek EAP services for a variety of reasons, often involving problems pertaining to mental health, relationships at home and at work, substance abuse, legal or financial problems, and other stresses or crises.[61] Despite this, one third of employees who make use of use EAPs undergo a formal referral process, a third of EAPs include a mandatory use component, and fewer than one in ten companies link drug testing to their EAPs.[62]

Team and group level

Performance in an organisation is also dependent on a team or group effort. The introduction of EAPs for groups (departments, sections, labour unions and other bodies that represent employees) is of the utmost importance. EAPs were historically introduced to eliminate suspicion and mistrust of management's motives towards labour unions. The unions' positive motives and their desire to promote employees' health have contributed to the successful introduction of

EAPs at both the group and the team level. It is in the interests of its members that unions are encouraged to participate in EAPs to promote workplace safety, rehabilitation, and disciplinary action in cases of drug abuse. Labour unions, however, prefer to sponsor their own EAPs so as to remain independent and avoid being excluded or dominated by management on issues relating to programme development.[63]

In addition to the above roles and functions, the following pertain to EAPs at the group or team level:

- Contributing to efforts to humanise the workplace for groups.
- Meeting the needs of a changing work environment.
- Meeting the needs of changing workforce teams.
- Helping to improve employee-team work performance.
- Containing and reducing organisational costs in relation to attending to employee-team challenges and problems such as acclimatisation, absenteeism, discrimination and substance abuse.
- Meeting team health and general wellbeing needs.
- Helping to maintain and increase team work commitment and loyalty.
- Helping the organisation with evaluation and feedback about the reactions of groups on a variety of issues.
- Improving general management-team relations.
- Meeting the legal and social responsibilities which organisations have towards teams.

Organisational level

The establishment of EAPs at an organisational level represents a major paradigm shift in terms of how troubled employees are viewed. It is through the establishment of EAPs that most organisations are starting to value the treatment and rehabilitation of such employees and workers. Organisations are also able to present themselves as socially responsible by incorporating EAPs into their long-term plans.

At this level, EAPs are effective in helping troubled employees to engage fully, be it in terms of their work contribution or their personal lives. Management teams frequently adopt EAPs for the good of business. The effective use of EAPs, as well as the training and skills they offer, can help supervisors recognise, identify and confront the problems their employees face;[64] it is another way of ensuring that organisations hold onto their skilled workforce.[65] EAPs can also proactively reduce an organisation's medical scheme spending on mental illness, i.e., they are a valuable tool in addressing stress-related issues before they escalate into costly mental conditions.[66]

EAPs at an organisational level:
• help organisations to restore valuable employees to full productivity; • assist in emphasising the organisation's commitment to valuing its employees by demonstrating concern for their welfare; • are useful in helping to draw up policies relating to alcohol and drug use and abuse; • enable managers and supervisors to offer staff something positive to address personal issues affecting their performance; • effect saving on medical costs, as the number of claims decreases when such programmes are implemented; and • allow organisations to get to know how employees react to issues of change and corporate policy.

Organisations can achieve their objectives as they pertain to productivity or services by means of different types of behaviour and interaction aimed at supporting employees. The more congruent the behaviour and interactions in terms of the objectives, the more effective the results. Problems are frequently caused by management's tendency to be so concerned with technical processes that they are perceived to be insensitive to the complex "human factors", social and behavioural transactions, and processes which constantly affect business objectives and outcomes.

EAP interventions are necessary for facilitating changes to, or the development of, processes in the social-technical structure of an organisation, that is, in the physical work environment and amongst employees. Select interventions may target work environments, group or individual behaviour, or even the development of specific skills. Organisational behaviour and processes mostly include leadership; supervision; communication; group relations; the handling of conflict; decision-making processes; problem solving; planning and the setting of objectives; group and meeting processes; interpersonal relationships; evaluation and control processes; and criticism and renewal processes.

In addition to the above, Mogorosi[67] indicated that the roles of EAP practitioners at the organisational level are to:

- serve as liaisons between the executive leadership and employees on matters pertaining to employees' welfare/wellness and organisational development;
- inform and advise employees on issues that have an impact on their work, their wellbeing and their careers;
- make an assessment of each individual's personal, social and economic environment, as it is likely to affect his/her functioning, productivity and personal growth;

- provide professional counselling, assistance, advice and referral to employees on identified areas of personal concern;
- identify and form resource linkages with community and professional service providers on employee problems and needs;
- encourage discussions around and create a focus on identified employee problems, concerns and needs; and
- improve and further research into identified employee problems, concerns and needs.

Given their massive scope, many regard EAPs as a workplace panacea for both personal and professional issues, which are guaranteed to enhance outcomes for employees and organisations.[68] A study by Grobler and Joubert[69] of 37,816 SAPS employees found that EAPs are indeed fulfilling management's obligation to ensure the health and wellness of their employees, but they are not a cure-all.

CONCLUSION

This chapter offered some insight into EAPs as a concept and a multi-faceted professional field. The historical development of such programmes should provide practitioners and managers with insight into the coming-into-being of EAPs in both the local and international contexts. EAPs play a valuable role and perform a vital function in enhancing work adjustment at the individual, group and organisational levels. The following chapter will focus more closely on the needs analysis and scope of practice for EAPs.

Chapter 2

EAP NEEDS ANALYSIS AND SCOPE OF PRACTICE

INTRODUCTION

When planning EAPs as a practitioner or manager, it is important to start by conducting a needs assessment. The purpose of this chapter is twofold: first, the focus is on the different types of diagnostic tools and processes for conducting an EAP needs assessment and analysis at the different levels of an organisation; and second, the principles and scope of EAPs are explored as proactive and reactive systems for managing the work dysfunctions of employees and groups.

WHAT IS A NEEDS ASSESSMENT?

Kaufman and Guerra-Lopez[70] defined a need as the gap between the results obtained and those that are desired, and also focused on the consequences of that gap. A needs assessment is therefore the process of identifying the gap between what is and what is to be. In the present context, the needs assessment process is aimed at comparing costs and aligning them with the purpose of the proposed programme.

Needs analysis and diagnosis refer to methods that are focused on understanding the organisational content, on identifying the elements of the organisation and their nature, as well as the relations between them.[71] The purpose of an EAP needs analysis is, first, to identify the rationale behind using EAPs, and second, to clarify the mechanisms by which EAPs are used in organisations.[72]

Several benefits can be derived from conducting an EAP needs assessment, including the following:[73]

- It provides an external, objective check to the subjective process of planning an EAP.
- It can identify problem areas in which EAP services may be cost-effective.
- The composition of the workforce in terms of age, sex and marital status, for example, may indicate the need for different types of services.
- It can identify barriers to the use of an EAP, which can be addressed prior to implementing services.
- The information can serve as a benchmark for determining if and how well the programme is working.

- It provides information on the size and scope of the relationship between job performance and personal problems.
- It can provide an estimate of the savings that can be produced by having an EAP.

In their research on the SAPS, Grobler and Joubert[74] discovered that many inaccurate opinions, misconceptions and myths exist regarding the need for, and experiences of, EAPs and their associated services. This implies that a needs analysis process must be followed to diagnose and assess the purpose of any EAP. An organisational diagnosis should provide the answer to the following questions: 1) Why should any organisation have an EAP?; and 2) What should the content of the EAP include, for example, what should the focus area of an EAP in an organisation be? The main role of a needs analysis is to provide an understanding of the organisation and determine the effectiveness of any actions taken by that organisation, by simplifying the reality.

An EAP needs analysis can assist the organisation to determine its focus areas. It is helpful to begin by identifying the purpose of EAPs and the ways in which such interventions can be used in modern organisations. This will clarify why and how EAPs are implemented to influence workplaces.[75] An analysis entails a process whereby practitioners collect information from organisational stakeholders (employees and management); disseminate their findings; and make recommendations to the organisation on how to improve performance.[76] Most organisations need EAPs for a variety of reasons (see Table 2.1).

Table 2.1: The need for EAPs in organisations

To improve	**To reduce**	**To manage**	**To help with**
Success	Litigation	Change	Policy implementation
Morale	Costs	Problem people	Counselling
Commitment	Absenteeism	Stress	Downsizing
Performance	Staff turnover	Uncertainty	Reactions to a crisis
Profits	Accidents	Environment	Specific needs or events
Productivity	Withdrawal		Problem diagnosis
Quality	Conflict		Problem expression
Image/PR	Stress		Problem dissipation
Perks	Anxiety		Problem solution
Benefit package			
Feedback			
Coping skills			
Health			

Source: Public Service Commission (2006)

A needs analysis of EAPs determines the effectiveness of workplace health promotion from both an individual and an organisational health perspective. There is mounting evidence of the value of EAPs in positively influencing employees' health and wellbeing via changes to their health behaviours.[77] One study found that while EAPs were generally effective in reducing anxiety, stress, depression and absenteeism, they only had a moderate impact on heightening job commitment, improving work functioning, increasing job satisfaction and preventing substance misuse.[78] Offering EAPs to employees is seen as a way of curtailing some of the crossover between work and personal domains, by assisting employees to deal with the issues at hand. Nair and Xavier[79] stated that an EAP can help create a peaceful workspace and enhance employees' skills in meeting all the challenges they might face in their personal or professional lives. This is in addition to decreasing financial costs, reducing employee turnover and absenteeism, and preventing burnout and accident-related disabilities.

THE STEPS IN AN EAP NEEDS ASSESSMENT

As the global increase in chronic lifestyle diseases continues to place a burden on individuals and organisations, so notable interest in, and the need for, EAPs in the workplace have increased. The process of conducting a needs assessment involves a variety of data collection methods and steps. Daniels[80] outlined the following:

Step 1 Organise a survey to identify current problems and concerns, as well as the need for an EAP.

Step 2 Define and draw up the exact shape and requirements of the EAP.

Step 3 Identify and evaluate the external providers of EAPs against the aforementioned requirements and create a shortlist of those that are considered suitable.

Step 4 For internally designed EAPs, the use of an external consultant is required to provide support with its establishment and to assist with advertising and recruiting managers and counsellors.

Step 5 Once the EAP is up and running, perform annual audits to improve the programme's effectiveness and report to management.

To establish an EAP initiative, Mogorosi[81] stated that the processes of programme development and a needs analysis involve the following necessary steps and activities:

- The establishment of a small work group to investigate the initiative of establishing such a programme.
- Institutional profiling (organisational type, staff profile and complement, jobs profiles).

- A survey of employee behaviour and actions in relation to patterns of absenteeism, sick leave, and disciplinary and grievance cases.
- A needs assessment study of typical problems, needs and organisational challenges.
- Consultation with all institutional stakeholders (staff, unions, management).
- Benchmarking with similar institutions and other organisations.
- The development of policies and structures.
- The conceptualisation of the programme staff, profile and job duties.
- Presentation of the final report of recommendations to institutional management.

Any needs analysis should take careful consideration of organisational dynamics into account, such as operational structures, staff composition, diverse needs and fluctuating budgets.[82] The needs analysis process is critical, as it provides an understanding of the nature and uniqueness of the work environment of each organisation, and should thus focus on the following elements:

- Profiles of employees.
- Profiles of customers/clients.
- Work environment and structure.
- Employee relations or labour relations records.
- Employee challenges and problems.
- Organisational competitiveness.

DATA COLLECTION AND ANALYSIS PROCESS

The process of data collection can make use of qualitative and quantitative research methods to deliver both primary and secondary data; the former refers to original data collected for a specific goal or purpose, while the latter are data originally collected for a different purpose, before being reused for another goal.

Qualitative data collection and analysis

As an approach, qualitative data collection is descriptive in nature, i.e., it is concerned with the meaning that individuals attach to things or events in their lives. Leedy[83] described this approach as being characterised by the collection of subjective data from a small sample of participants. There are a variety of methods of data collection in qualitative research, including observation, textual or visual analysis (from books or videos) and interviews (individual or group).[84]

There are three fundamental types of ***qualitative research interviews***: structured, semi-structured and unstructured:[85]

- Structured interviews are essentially verbally administered questionnaires, in which lists of predetermined questions are asked with little or no variation, and with no scope for follow-up questions to responses that warrant elaboration. Consequently, they are relatively quick and easy to administer, and may be of particular use in clarifying specific questions. They are ideal to use if respondents are likely to experience problems with literacy or numeracy. However, by their very nature, such interviews only allow for limited participant responses, and are therefore of little value if "depth" is required.
- Semi-structured interviews consist of several key questions that help to define the areas to be explored, but also allow the interviewer or interviewee to diverge in order to pursue an idea or response in greater detail. This interview format is used most frequently, as it provides participants with some guidance on what to talk about, which many find helpful. The flexibility of this approach, particularly compared to structured interviews, is that it allows for the discovery or elaboration of information that is important to participants, but may not previously have been deemed pertinent by the interviewer/researcher.
- Unstructured interviews do not reflect any preconceived theories or ideas and are performed with little or no prearrangement. Such interviews may simply start with an opening question such as the following: "Tell me about your expectations of EAP professionals." The interview will progress based primarily on the respondent's initial response. Unstructured interviews are usually very time-consuming, often lasting several hours. They can be difficult to manage and just as difficult to participate in. The lack of predetermined interview questions provides little guidance on what to talk about – something many participants find confusing and unhelpful. Their use is, therefore, generally only considered where significant "depth" is required, where virtually nothing is known about the subject area, or where a different perspective is sought on a known subject area.

Focus groups offer another means of collecting qualitative data during the needs analysis process. A focus group entails a group discussion on a particular topic, organised for research purposes. This method is used for generating information on collective views and the meanings underlying those views,[86] and are useful for generating a rich understanding of participants' experiences and beliefs. Focus groups share many common features with less structured interviews, but there is more to them than merely collecting similar data from many participants at once.

Any such structured discussions must be guided, monitored and recorded by the researcher (in this context, the EAP practitioner or human resource development specialist tasked with doing the needs analysis). Worldwide, researchers employ focus groups to explore a range of phenomena. The primary goal in choosing this method is to use the data resulting from discussions or interactions among participants (such as questioning one another, commenting on their experiences) to increase the depth of the inquiry and unveil aspects of a phenomenon assumed to be otherwise less accessible.[87] While there are positives to using focus groups during a needs analysis, there are also negatives (see Table 2.2).

Interviews and focus group methods can be combined during a needs analysis. Broadly speaking there are three rationales for doing so: pragmatic reasons, the need to compare and contrast participants' perspectives (parallel use), and striving for data completeness.[88] Qualitative data are mainly analysed according to ***themes and subthemes***, through which common trends are identified and grouped into related themes. The aim of such an analysis is to consolidate the narrated data obtained from the interviews and focus group recordings or notes.

Table 2.2 indicates the strengths and challenges of this data collection method.

Table 2.2: Focus group strengths and challenges

Strengths	**Challenges**
• It is comparatively easier to conduct. • It allows the researcher to explore topics and generate hypotheses. • It presents an opportunity to collect data from the group interaction, which concentrates on the topic the researcher is interested in. • It has high "face validity" (data). • It costs less than most other methods. • It delivers speedy results (in terms of evidence of the group meeting). • It allows the researcher to increase the size of the sample of his/her qualitative study.	• It is not conducted in a natural atmosphere. • The researcher has less control over the data generated. • Data analysis is more difficult. Group interaction creates a social atmosphere and any comments should be interpreted in this context. • It demands that interviewers be carefully trained. • It takes effort to assemble groups. • The atmosphere should be conducive to dialogue.

Sources: Krueger (1994); Morgan (1988)

In the South African context, it is worthwhile for managers and facilitators to investigate the use of group techniques such as World Café and Appreciative Inquiry[89] to involve employees of all demographic groups, of all qualifications and at all job levels, regardless of their respective years of service.

Quantitative data collection and analysis

According to Wellman, Kruger and Mitchell,[90] a quantitative approach is used to gather data from large groups, such as a representative cross-section of staff in a large organisation, or from a large group of employees. It involves objective data collection by means of questionnaires, surveys, instruments and inventories.

A ***survey*** is simply a data collection tool for carrying out research. This quantitative method can be used to conduct an EAP needs analysis. To this end, the organisation might host the survey, or it might make use of a service provider to handle the survey hosting, administration and reporting services.[91]

Surveys are ideal in that they have the following strengths:

- They provide breadth over depth.
- They require large samples, thus data are more readily generalised.
- They are standardised, but do not allow for the exploration of answers in depth.
- They can be relatively simple to analyse, but yield less rich data.
- Minimal sampling errors occur due to the relatively low cost per survey.

In terms of survey limitations, they are generally unsuitable where an understanding of the historical context of a phenomenon is required.[92] In addition, biases may occur during the data analysis process due to a lack of response from the intended participants, or problems with the nature and accuracy of the responses received. Other sources of error include respondents intentionally misreporting behaviours in order to confound the survey results or hide inappropriate behaviour. Finally, respondents may have difficulty assessing their own behaviours or may have poor recall of the circumstances surrounding their actions. It is important to take cognisance of the ethical considerations pertaining to survey participation; one such consideration is recognising that participation is voluntary, i.e., the researcher should encourage participation without exerting undue pressure or coercing the respondents.[93]

Questionnaires or instruments normally form part of surveys as they require minimal resources (staff, time and cost) and are best suited to eliciting confidential information. There are also minimal interviewer and respondent measurement errors due to the absence of direct contact. Martins and Ledimo[94] indicated that the two main methods of data collection via a quantitative questionnaire are web-based (which requires a computer or smart phone and internet access) and paper-based. The process allows the respondent the greatest latitude in terms of the pace and sequence of responses.[95] With regard to the challenges posed by questionnaires and instruments, they are typically subject to non-response error. Less educated, illiterate and disabled people in particular are less likely to respond to questionnaires, which are also subject to bias where the intended respondent refers to others in completing the survey. Finally, questionnaires and instruments are subject to item non-response where certain questions may be inadvertently or intentionally skipped.

Quantitative data are mainly analysed using descriptive and interferential statistics. Descriptive statistics involve frequencies, means, percentages, validity and reliability measures, while correlation, variance, factor and regression analyses are the inferential statistics which are applicable to quantitative data analysis.[96] In summary, Table 2.3 presents the differences between the qualitative and quantitative approaches.

Table 2.3: Differences between the qualitative and quantitative approaches

Dimensions	Qualitative	Quantitative
Evaluations	Deals with subjective data.	Evaluates objective data.
Focus	Focus is flexible and exploratory. Focus is more on the validity and representation of the data.	Focus is complex and structured, and tests hypotheses. Focus is on the reliability of the data and measuring instrument.
Methods	Interviews, observer-as-participant observation, focus groups, documents and archival data.	Questionnaires, surveys, instruments and inventories.
Investigation	Conducts the investigation to achieve an insider's view.	Conducts the investigation from the outsider's perspective.
Process	Process is dynamic and changeable.	Process is stable in nature.
Approach	Data collection is wide, hence the approach is holistic.	Data collection is structured, hence the approach is particularistic.
Sample	Collects data from small sample groups.	Collects data using large samples.

Source: Martins and Ledimo (2017)

Needs analysis report

The purpose of a needs analysis, in the context of an EAP, is for the practitioner as researcher to be able to share their findings about the feasibility of such an intervention with relevant parties in the organisation. The following are the key elements that should form part of any needs analysis report:

- Title.
- Purpose and aims.
- Background and motivation.
- Data collection process (with an overview of the research approach, data collection method and sampling procedure).
- Data analysis and presentation of results (depending on the choice of data collection method).
- Recommendation and conclusions (to support or veto the implementation of an EAP).
- Limitations of the needs analysis findings.

It is important to keep the report short, because most executives and managers prefer concise documents. The language used should be accurate and easy to read – using language that is difficult to understand may create confusion and misunderstandings. Some organisations require a PowerPoint presentation of the report, which is helpful when giving an overview of the analysis results during a feedback session.

SCOPE OF EAPs

The scope of EAPs is infinite, as they reflect the needs of a wide range of organisations.[97] Currently, the scope of the services offered by EAPs is influenced by market pressures, rather than a systematic identification and validation of the key attributes of an effective programme. A programme can, however, be limited by a practitioner's lack of creativity in thinking up new ideas and novel benefits. There is still some confusion with regard to the terms of standardisation, measurement, evaluation and, most importantly, quality improvement. This uncertainty is compounded by the lack of minimum professional credentials and programme standards required to provide EAP-related services. As a result, most interventions are presented by trained persons from diverse academic and non-academic backgrounds.

Employee assessment, counselling and therapeutic services

To counteract the negative impact that mental health problems have on business, organisations are increasingly investing in mental health promotion, prevention and intervention efforts.[98] It is a fundamental principle that EAPs exist to assess employees' work dysfunction and provide counselling services.

Employee assessment, which is the initial aspect of providing services to employees, requires the thoughtful definition of any dysfunction or maladjustment in a confidential manner. It is a method of collecting in-depth information about an employee's social situation and his/her physical, mental and psychological functioning across diverse areas. Interviews and psychological tests can be used to collect and analyse information, diagnose the employee's situation and then establish goals for intervention. This process of an EAP assessment entails the identification and evaluation of an employee's strengths, weaknesses, problems and needs.[99]

During the assessment, the EAP practitioner assumes the role of counsellor. In this role s/he should be able to take a detailed look at the nature and severity of the employee's situation. To arrive at a comprehensive picture, the employee's manager or next of kin can also be interviewed. It is upon completion of this assessment that the counsellor and employee will discuss which options appear to be most realistic in terms of helping the employee resolve the situation s/he is grappling with.

Counselling services are critical in EAPs. As a counsellor, the EAP practitioner is able to address certain work-related maladjustments or dysfunctions immediately. One of the goals of the pioneers of EAP was to have workplace counselling be provided as an employee benefit.[100] There are times when the employee will choose the treatment on offer, and a referral, if necessary, will be arranged. If this is not the chosen route, employee counselling in the workplace is another option; this is gaining prominence and has become increasingly important with incidents of stress-related health issues being on the rise.[101] An improvement in employee performance increases productivity, thus the organisation can achieve a competitive advantage through encouraging employee counselling.

Counselling services are offered as a process through which a client or employee who has a problem receives personal assistance during a private discussion(s). Counselling, which involves a structured conversation aimed at improving the employee's quality of life in the face of adversity, is a generic term used to cover processes such as interviewing, guiding and advising.[102] With an increase in incidences of traumatic events at work, including workplace violence and natural disasters, employers are relying more on their EAP practitioners to provide crisis intervention and short-term counselling.[103] Employee counselling mostly focuses on issues such as self-understanding, decision-making, goal setting, planning for the future and managing interpersonal problems. According to Nair and Xavier,[104] the main objective is to help individuals become self-sufficient, self-reliant and self-directed, and to help them adjust efficiently so that they can lead a meaningful life.

Therapeutic services, within the scope of EAPs, see professionals with expertise providing therapy to assist employees to deal with their situation post-assessment. According to Rakepa,[105] therapeutic services are intended to treat those mental and psychological problems that affect the full functioning of individual employees. This occurs once the therapist has completed his/her assessment and diagnosis of the employee, and is able to provide or recommend the appropriate intervention. Some organisations may not have an EAP practitioner who is qualified as a therapist, hence referral is an important part of the scope of practice in this field.

Hanisch, Birner, Oberhauser, Nowak and Sabariego[106] confirmed that many organisations have implemented EAPs, which typically offer assessment, counselling and referral services to employees with work-related or personal problems. Thus, EAPs are touted as assisting employees to return to routine tasks by minimising the loss of productive work time, preventing premature retirement, and increasing the productivity levels of injured employees.[107] EAPs exist to assist employees garner the necessary resources to manage the multiple (and sometimes conflicting) demands of work and family life.[108]

EAPs as a support service to managers and supervisors

Managers and supervisors are often faced with the challenge of creating an ideal work environment for employees. Due to the complexity of managing and supervising employees, they frequently require the support of EAP professionals to help them fulfil their role. According to Joseph and Walker,[109] another frequently used EAP service is "manager assist", which is a management coaching service. Most managers and supervisors in industry lead others based on their professional expertise as engineers or technicians, for example, i.e., their limited expertise in people management leads them to require the help and support of EAPs to enable them to lead staff who face work dysfunctions.

According to Govender,[110] South African EAPs essentially evolved due to changing social and legislative conditions within the workplace, but the current driver of EAPs is the recognition that the system can play a key role in supporting employees and managers to manage their work-life stressors, or any behavioural, health and physical risks arising out of the transformation process unfolding in ever-evolving organisations.

Over the years, organisations have come to realise the value of the EAP services offered to employees, supervisors and managers alike. For this reason, they provide access to EAPs to help people deal with the numerous physical, emotional, mental and social challenges that impact on their performances as employees.[111] The cost of an unhealthy workforce translates into absenteeism, decreased productivity, reduced focus at work and stressful behaviours – these challenges have led employers across the globe to realise that there is a need to intervene.[112] Supervisors and managers can receive training from EAP practitioners within the organisation about the scope and intent of a particular programme. As this type of training is essential for maintaining the efficiency of an EAP, a highly effective programme practitioner must take the time to train and consult with supervisors on a continuous basis.[113]

EAPs can provide support to an organisation's management and leadership in the following areas:[114]

- Help to reduce labour turnover resulting from unresolved problems experienced by the employee in question, which could have been amicably dealt with and resolved whilst the worker remained productive and an asset within the organisation.
- Assisting with change and transformation taking place as a result of socio-political changes.
- Assisting employees to comprehend the cause and effect of change and to harness a coping mechanism with the rationalisation process by dealing with the trauma of sudden changes in jobs or skills requirements, relocation, cultural shock and basic resistance to change.
- Assisting with low morale and demotivation, communication problems and work performance issues that occur as a result of the above.

Joseph and Walker[115] argued that EAP services should offer mediation, facilitation, debriefing, training, coaching, mentoring, redundancy and/or outplacement services to employees. In addition, Dawad and Hoque[116] stated that EAPs are a critical component of any credible talent management strategy, the benefits of which include reduced absenteeism, increased presenteeism, adherence to labour legislation requirements, improved industrial relations, increased employee performance and productivity, reduced healthcare costs, and a reduction in the number of workplace accidents.

EAP services to the organisation

The scope of EAP services is not limited to the employee, management and supervisory support discussed above; EAP services play a critical role in helping the organisation realise its strategic objectives. The mandate of every business is to be efficient, effective and profitable, hence organisations have to manage risks to their operations as these arise from employees experiencing work dysfunction.[117] This has encouraged the establishment of comprehensive EAPs in the manufacturing, construction, mining, educational and government sectors, amongst others.

Crisis management is a critical service that can be offered at an organisational level to deal with a critical incident. Organisations are faced with many risks on a daily basis – certain of these may even threaten the lives of individual employees. A critical incident or trauma is any situation that causes the employee to experience a strong emotional reaction, and critical incident management support should thus include post-incident on-site and off-site debriefings, follow-up face-to-face or telephone counselling, and trauma training.[118]

Crisis management has the potential to interfere with an employee's ability to function effectively. During such difficult times in an organisation, an EAP practitioner's role is to provide a psychological debriefing and to empower individuals/groups who have undergone traumatic experiences.[119] Jacobson,[120] in focusing on workplace violence, indicated that critical incident response models should include preventative training and risk assessment, immediate response for victims, individual assessment and support, group intervention, management consultation, and post-incident response intervention and evaluation.

Prevention programmes can be implemented to support the organisation, yet most interventions aim to promote employee mental health by focusing on the individual (e.g. teaching stress management techniques) while neglecting the organisation as a whole (stressful working conditions). However, many factors that positively affect employee mental health are related to the social environment at work, such as the working culture, the level of social support and the leadership style.[121] According to Kunte,[122] there is evidence to suggest that multi-component health promotion and risk reduction programmes can permanently change lifestyle habits and reduce health risks amongst employees.

Nair and Xavier[123] argued that with the mounting pressures of work and life, it is imperative that organisations become more proactive than reactive: in these fast-paced times, the eventualities of mind and body are quite unpredictable. Rakepa[124] indicated that prevention programmes in organisations entail systematic patterns of activities that EAP professionals can use to bring about change in groups or individuals. This includes awareness or training programmes that empower groups and divisions within the organisation with relevant life skills aimed at enhancing their performance and productivity. In their study of the SAPS (a sample of almost 40,000 employees), Grobler and Joubert[125] found that EAP practitioners should continue to develop and implement needs-based, flexible and readily available (non-exclusive) proactive intervention approaches. Thus, such services assist employees by helping them to alleviate problems, aiding in their recuperation and making them more productive members of the workforce.[126]

PRINCIPLES OF EAPs

EAPs function on basic principles that govern their implementation in organisations. The following are critical principles in the effective and successful initiation, planning and execution of EAPs:

- Management and unions working together can help employees deal with personal or work-related stressors which would otherwise lead to deteriorating work performance.
- The EAP applies equally to all employees.
- The EAP respects the confidentiality and privacy of information.

- The EAP encourages employees to voluntarily seek help for personal problems which may affect their job performance.
- The EAP offers assistance for a wide range of problems which may include physical, emotional, marital or familial distress; legal or financial problems; various addictions; issues of harassment; job-related stress or job conflict.
- The supervisor or manager is responsible for identifying an employee whose job performance is below standard, not for diagnosing a personal problem. The EAP practitioner works with management and unions to offer early intervention using wellness programming in the workplace.
- The EAP recognises the need to grant employees or employers leave for the purposes of counselling and/or treatment.

In support of the above, Mogorosi[127] argued that an EAP should be guided by the following three basic principles:

Principle I: An EAP is a job-based strategy for helping employees solve their problems

At some stage during their work-life, it should be expected that employees, like everyone else, will experience problems – either personal or related to work. The very recognition of this fact will go a long way in helping to establish harmonious relations between management and employees. When an employee's problems affect his/her work performance, the organisation has an obligation to offer help.

Employees with problems have the right to resolve them in a way they see fit. There are certain problems, however, that may have an effect on, or spill over into, work performance (e.g. absenteeism and addiction). At that point the organisation can offer help; it is assumed that employees' problems are private unless they cause job performance to deteriorate. When personal problems become a matter of concern for the organisation, the manager will have to use EAPs to protect the organisation's most valuable asset – the trained employee.

Principle II: Constructive confrontation is used to motivate employees to resolve their problems and overcome denial

One important duty of any manager or supervisor is to see to it that work is done appropriately. Whenever work performance is seen to deteriorate, it is management's duty to help an employee correct that. Organisations need to have disciplinary and grievance procedures in place, through which supervisors and managers can "confront" employees about their poor work performance, should it continue.

Employees may either acknowledge their problems, deny their existence, or may be unaware of their performance being below standard. Through a "constructive confrontation" process, supervisors and managers might discuss poor work performance and how best to reverse the situation. This can be done by suggesting that the employee concerned seek help from the programme. Relying on EAP services should never be seen as a means of avoiding disciplinary procedures. One of the possible outcomes of a failure to deal with such problems is having to take disciplinary action against non-performing employees. Constructive confrontation helps supervisors and managers focus solely on job performance; they should refrain from making a diagnosis of the problems by themselves.

Principle III: Counselling is used to help employees solve their problems, when it is clear that these problems are beyond the employees' control

The third principle states that EAP policies need to reflect an undertaking that employees will be helped to work through their problems, when both the employee and the organisation agree that some action is necessary. For their part, employees are expected to rely on their own solutions and resources to maintain their independence. When an employee's resources have been exhausted and his/her problems are beyond their control, outside help may be called in – including the help of the employing organisation.

EAP principles according to the Employee Assistance Professionals Association (EAPA)

The EAPA, as an international professional body for EAP practitioners and professionals, has developed a set of professional principles and ethics, based on specialised knowledge, to define the characteristics of an EAP. These are the fundamental assumptions associated with those rules of behaviour that are necessary when implementing a code of conduct.[128]

Stated below are some of the professional principles developed by the EAPA:[129]

- Consult, train, and assist organisational leaders (managers, supervisors, and union stewards) who are seeking to manage a troubled employee, enhance the work environment, and improve employee job performance.
- Outreach/educate employees/dependents about the availability of Employee Assistance (EA) services.
- Confidential and timely problem identification/assessment services for employee clients with personal concerns that may affect job performance.
- Use constructive confrontation, motivation, and short-term interventions with employee clients to address problems that affect job performance.

- Refer employee clients for diagnosis, treatment and assistance, plus case monitoring and follow-up services.
- Assist organisations to manage provider contracts, and form and audit relations with service providers, managed care organisations, insurers, and other third party payers.
- Assist organisations to support employee health benefits covering medical/behavioural problems, including but not limited to, alcoholism, drug abuse, and mental/emotional disorders.
- Identify the effects of EAP services on an organisation and individual job performance.

EAPS principles according to the Employee Assistance Professionals Association of South Africa (EAPA-SA)

At a national level, the EAPA-SA has outlined a number of principles in a code of conduct which is applicable to professionals in this field. These principles align with those of the EAPA (discussed above).

In terms of the EAPA-SA, the following principles should distinguish EAPs from other workplace programmes:[130]

- Training and development of managers, supervisors and unions in order to effectively manage those employees who experience behavioural, emotional and wellness issues, so as to enhance the work environment and employee performance.
- Guarantee confidentiality to management, supervisors, unions, employees and their family members.
- Case management for employees with personal and work-related problems that affect their job performance through confidentiality and timely risk identification, assessment, motivation, short-term intervention, referral, monitoring, follow-up, reintegration and aftercare services.
- Consultation services to organisations in order to address inherent trends arising from personal or organisational issues.
- Network with internal and external role-players as well as service providers in order to establish and maintain relations.
- Monitor and evaluate the value, success and impact of the services provided to organisations and individuals.

CONCLUSION

This chapter explained the importance and benefits of conducting a needs analysis for an EAP within the organisation. By studying the various data collection and analysis processes using qualitative and quantitative methods, the practitioner should be able to make a choice from the relevant methods. Keep in mind that the purpose of a needs analysis is to share the relevant findings in a report or feedback session. This chapter provided an indication of the scope of practice for EAP practitioners at the employee, management and organisational levels respectively. This scope should assist both practitioners and managers to determine their focus and the limitations of their respective roles. Knowledge of the principles of EAP is essential for understanding the codes or standards that govern the role of practitioners in this field, before embarking on the implementation process.

Chapter 3

INITIATION OF AN EAP

INTRODUCTION

The initiation of EAPs in organisations is based on a theoretical model adopted to deal with work dysfunctions and maladjustments. This chapter guides practitioners in the field in focusing on both reactive and proactive approaches. The service delivery models initiated can be either internal (in-house), external (outsourced) or comprehensive in nature. This chapter concludes by focusing on the comprehensive identification, allocation and management of the human and financial resources necessary for the successful implementation of EAPs.

WORK ADJUSTMENT, MALADJUSTMENT AND DYSFUNCTION

EAPs can be defined as initiatives aimed at enhancing the wellbeing and performance of employees, hence their role and function are mainly to address work maladjustments and dysfunctions, in order to effect work adjustment.

The concepts "adjustment", "maladjustment" and "dysfunction" in the work context can be defined as follows:

- Work adjustment refers to an employee's wellbeing in the work context. It implies that s/he is in a healthy state – psychologically, physically, socially and spiritually – to fulfil a specific role. Such an employee does not demonstrate behaviour which is usually attributed to recognised patterns of abnormal behaviour, and s/he has the ability to cope effectively with life's demands in various life roles, and to realise his/her potential within certain expectations.
- Work dysfunction refers to an employee's inability to perform due to ill health or abnormal behaviour. Work-related problems or work dysfunctions can, however, be work-specific, and may be based on certain job-related attitudes, ethics and values – conditions which may not necessarily be easily definable or diagnosable.
- Maladjustment in the workplace applies to behaviour that is usually diagnosable, given recognised abnormal behaviour or patterns of behaviour which cause the employee to be unable to cope with life's requirements as expected, or as deemed the norm in various life roles.

Work dysfunctions are evident in a pattern analysis of withdrawal behaviour that may confirm an employee's progressive disengagement. Another indicator is a working style which reflects his/her inability to meet all the requirements of someone who is productive in a specific job or role. Such behaviour – classified as a work dysfunction or work performance impairment – implies that the cause may lie with the employee (e.g. emotional problems), or may be attributable to the interaction between the employee and the work environment. Repeated instances of work dysfunction clearly call for an EAP intervention, but some employees may require assistance in managing related concerns in respect of interpersonal relations, job design, work pressure and how to handle their emotions.[131]

Mogorosi[132] listed a number of symptoms of employee work dysfunction or maladjustment, i.e., increased absenteeism, unexpected vacation requests, sporadic and erratic work performance, tardiness and missed deadlines, increased strife with co-workers and supervisors, loss of enthusiasm for work, unpredictable behaviour patterns/moodiness, increased complaints, above-average work accident rates, costly errors and difficulties in following instructions.

Withdrawal behaviour, as a dysfunction or maladjustment, is not indicative of an employee choosing to be or remaining at a specific workplace voluntarily. Their choices indicate a misfit or non-fit between employee and organisation, in that the employee prefers to escape from an unsatisfying job or work relationship. Many personal attributes (such as self-esteem, self-actualisation, needs and expectations) exert a significant major influence in terms of job motivation and work performance. Organisational withdrawal, which eventually results in an individual physically leaving the workplace, can be voluntary (expressed as lateness, absenteeism, personnel turnover, resignation, job change or retirement) or non-voluntary (which manifests as employees being laid off or dismissed by the organisation).

Another form of withdrawal is ***psychological absence*** (as opposed to physical withdrawal), which is reflected in attitudes and emotions such as dissatisfaction, a lack of commitment, "loafing" or idling, wasting time and day-dreaming. In other words, employees are present in the workplace, but merely as "silent partners" who still reap work benefits. The fact is, they do not enjoy their work or contribute wholeheartedly to meeting organisational goals. Destructive forms of this type of passive withdrawal may manifest themselves in drinking, drug abuse and malicious gossip at work, as well as retirement decisions that leave employees demotivated and far from actively involved in work activities.

Personnel turnover or a change in job is mostly preceded by a stated intention to leave the workplace, or by thoughts of leaving. Factors that may lead to personnel turnover include work attitudes (work commitment, job dissatisfaction) toward managerial practices, the quality and nature of working conditions, remuneration, workers' feelings about whether management is treating them fairly, and work group attitudes. Conditions such as anxiety, depression, neuroses, personality problems, alcohol and drug addiction, physical diseases and age can also contribute to personnel turnover.

Absenteeism refers to unscheduled non-attendance at the workplace or failure to attend work activities which employees are expected to attend. Stable periodic lateness can usually be coupled with leisure time activities, income trade-offs and family responsibilities, while random lateness is often the result of uncontrollable events such as accidents or transport problems. Absence from work, which could be a significant indicator of organisational stress, incurs great costs, especially in terms of lost productivity. Absenteeism or withdrawal behaviours could also be a manifestation of under-commitment, especially if this type of behaviour points to anti-organisational behaviour such as dishonesty, laziness and disloyalty.

Thus, it is argued that EAPs are able to improve employee morale, reduce healthcare costs, increase productivity, reduce absenteeism, and contribute to the positive promotion of the company's image.[133] Work stress is a serious problem for modern-day employees, with many reporting that work is a significant source of stress in their lives. This has myriad negative consequences, including burnout, decreased psychological wellbeing, and an increased risk of depression and/ or anxiety-related problems.[134]

DIFFERENT APPROACHES TO WORK ADJUSTMENT

As in other fields of study in psychology, "adjustment" implies that a number of broad and also more specific theoretical approaches can be used to explain or give meaning to the concept.

Scientific approach: this approach (on which this book is based) involves setting standards and developing methods for planning and carrying out measurement and research. Any description of the causes, symptoms and effects of treatment methods is reliant on theory, but also (more importantly) on verified assessment and research findings. In abnormal psychology or psychopathology, science is practiced by means of various well-known research procedures and assessment methods. Examples include genetic (family, sibling and twin) studies, observations done on experiments and in natural situations, surveys, questionnaires, clinical interviews, studies of historical and archival sources, physiological and neurological measurements, medical and health histories, work performance records, various types of psychological tests and the assessment of diverse environments.

Historical approach: people, events, philosophies, theories, research and ways of doing things in the past are still important for our understanding of the present stage of the theory and practice of psychopathology. A historical approach is used when someone's health status is assessed – it takes into account a person's past history of physical and psychological illness, as well as his/her interpersonal relationships, occupational history and family background.

Etiological approach: this approach stresses an identification of the causes or causality of maladjusted behaviour or psychopathological conditions. Etiology usually focuses on genetic (biological), psychosocial, cultural and external factors, but other frameworks can also be used.

This approach is used to study the principles of cause and effect, when attempting to explain adjustment.

Diagnostic approach: this makes provision for the identification and classification of functions which aim to distinguish and classify the symptoms and attributes of various clinical conditions (syndrome categories) according to certain criteria. The validity and method of diagnosis, as well as the criteria for diagnostic classification, are probably among the most controversial issues in psychopathology. Present-day psychopathologists, psychologists, social workers and medical health practitioners regard the Diagnostic and Statistical Manual of Mental Disorders (DSM-V, i.e., the 5th edition)[135] as the most appropriate classification, and it is widely used. A critical attitude towards the diagnosis of human behaviour is, however, always necessary, and other systems need to be used and researched.

Descriptive approach: this approach to abnormal behaviour is concerned with describing the distinctive illness processes, symptoms, characteristics and behavioural manifestations of various disorders. Clinical reports on clients, compiled after their assessment for diagnostic and prognostic purposes, are examples of descriptive explanations. This approach is also used to describe various illnesses, disorders and work dysfunctions.

Clinical or therapeutic approach (intervention approach): this approach is based on practically all the other approaches – especially the etiological, diagnostic and descriptive approaches. It is concerned with the prognosis of maladjustment, with methods of treating problems and with effecting health promotion, according to explanatory psychological approaches. Methods of clinical assessment, diagnosis and prognosis are normative, subjective, contextual and statistical in nature. They are based on external criteria such as personal judgements, speculations, biases, deviations from the norm, and statistical data. Certain aspects of these models are sometimes used positively, i.e., to communicate psychological adjustment or optimal health. A summary of these methods is outlined in Table 3.1.

[i] American Psychiatric Association. 2013. *Diagnostic and statistical manual of mental disorders: DSM-5*. Arlington, VA: American Psychiatric Association.

Table 3.1: Clinical approach assessment, diagnosis and prognosis methods

Types of methods	Nature of assessment, diagnosis and prognosis
Normative or ideal method	This method is based on the idea that a condition of perfection is the ideal form of behaviour. Religious/political figures, sportspeople, philosophers and others are examples of the models of such behaviour. This view of mental health is based on value judgements which may differ from one individual to the next, and on an ideal that is often scientifically unattainable. Moreover, idols have been proven, time and again, to have flaws – even psychological or criminal faults. The moral model is also based on the value judgements that educators and others make when describing behaviour as good or bad (e.g. when discussing responsible vs. irresponsible actions). In the legal model, deviant behaviour is judged in terms of certain rules and regulations, and behaviour is evaluated in terms of liability under the law.
Subjective method	In this model the individual as an employee is used as the norm to evaluate others as either normal or abnormal. There are many well-known examples of perceptual errors occurring when people are evaluated according to the assessor's personal preferences. These perceptual errors include the halo effect, prejudices and stereotypes, logical errors (the interviewer, in a situation where people have to be selected, classifies a client as a manipulator because the person displays verbal skills), mirror-image evaluations (the client has to resemble the interviewer, otherwise s/he is unsuitable), contrast errors (if the applicant is like the interviewer's boss, s/he will not be appointed), and the Yarvis effect (the therapist or interviewer will work/prefers to work only with people who are young, attractive, rich, verbally skilful, intelligent and socially skilled). These personal mental sets will influence assessment and counselling, especially in problem cases, which may mean that intervention is approached from an external frame of reference, while matters that are important to the troubled individual are ignored.

Types of methods	Nature of assessment, diagnosis and prognosis
Statistical method	In terms of this method, the average is regarded as normal and any deviation on either side of the scale is "abnormal" in some respects (this is the source of popular expressions like "the average worker", "average intelligence", etc.). Physical characteristics such as beauty, height and weight, and even psychological behaviours, are used to label people as measuring low, average or high on certain attributes. The normal distribution of intelligence is probably most relevant to our field, but it is difficult to explain psychological variables in terms of such a model. In many models, personality is expressed in matrices, for instance, a two-dimensional matrix of introversion-extroversion on one axis and normality and neuroticism on the other, or five or 16 bipolar factors. The question is whether "normality" is always the condition in-between the two poles, or in each of the five or 16 factors.
Contextual explanatory method	These methods, which are not necessarily psychological theories, emphasise the more or less complex interaction of employee attributes in the context of the work environment, and other surrounding environments and their attributes. Psychological concepts about human behaviour can be used within these approaches to explain health behaviours in context.

APPROACHES TO INITIATE AN EAP

An important principle of effective EAPs is that they need to be both reactive and proactive.[136] Organisations have found that it makes financial and business sense for EAPs to be reactive, proactive and preventive in their efforts to help employees identify and resolve personal issues before they have serious medical, familial, and/or workplace consequences.

Reactive approach

EAPs have historically been reactive rather than proactive, i.e., action is taken only after the problem has become apparent.[137] This implies that employees tend to be referred by their supervisors only after having failed to meet the required performance standards. A reactive approach to EAP thus usually occurs when it is self-initiated (i.e., by the employee): s/he recognises that a problem exists and seeks assistance by calling the EAP office directly. Alternatively, the action may have resulted from a co-worker, family member, friend or supervisor sharing his/her concerns about the employee, and informally suggesting that s/he make use of the EAP.

The Public Service Commission's evaluation of EAPs in the public sector indicates that such interventions are either absent or have a limited function within departments, and are generally reactive in respect of the manner in which they operate in the workplace.

A reactive approach to EAPs is described as follows:[138]

- They only deal with a very limited number of issues, i.e., some counselling.
- They have limited capacity and are often budget-starved.
- There are no high levels of visible management commitment to such units and they are often seen as a "nice to have".
- They only provide services upon request and therefore do not tackle workplace problems or potential workplace problems proactively.

Given the mounting pressures of balancing work and life, it is time that organisations became proactive, rather than reactive.

Proactive approach

EAPs act proactively when dealing with the workplace impacts of an employee's potential work dysfunctions. One reason for EAP professionals becoming involved could be that they are requested to do so by management or by an employee him/herself. The EAP office needs to have or develop a passion for helping people with specific problems, for instance by conducting programmes aimed at alleviating emotional trauma or dealing with substance abuse. A proactive approach which is aimed at employees has the potential to reach a large segment of the population who might otherwise not be exposed to health promotion initiatives.[139] According to Grobler and Joubert,[140] the primary focus of EAPs should be to undertake proactive interventions aimed at enhancing personal coping skills, thus enabling individuals to cope effectively with challenges that may arise, thereby improving their quality of life. An employee is responsible for keeping his/her job performance at an acceptable level; if it shows continuing deterioration and s/he rejects informal offers of assistance, then the supervisor may initiate a formal offer of assistance. Prior to doing so, the supervisor should consult with the EAP office concerning the appropriateness of the offer. This approach is proactive in that it is employer-initiated in nature. Pescud et al.[141] highlighted that this approach also provides practitioners with the opportunity to tailor programmes and health messages to the specific needs of industry segments and/or demographic groups.

The following steps govern an employer-initiated offer of assistance to an employee who shows work dysfunctions or maladjustment:

- Informal – the supervisor ensures that the employee receives an informal offer of assistance, prior to initiating a formal offer. Such offers must be documented. Note that certain dysfunctions could result in an employer-initiated offer(s) without prior informal offers having been made.
- Formal – the formal employer-initiated offer of assistance must appear in writing on a prescribed form, and must state the date and time of an appointment with the EAP professional. A formal offer of assistance can be hand delivered to the employee, with a copy being forwarded to the EAP professional and another copy retained in a confidential EAP file as a record that a formal offer of assistance was made.

The proactive approach is directed towards improving the health of a workforce through initiatives such as health risk assessments, vaccinations and wellness activities targeted at improving healthy eating, encouraging physical activity, limiting cigarette use and alcohol consumption, and promoting mental health outcomes.[142]

Comprehensive approach

Comprehensive EAPs are both reactive and proactive in nature; they involve employee counselling, support, awareness-raising and follow-ups. Such EAPs are very successful in efforts to provide assistance proactively to employees and in dealing with a wide range of problems. Pescud et al.[143] suggested that when it comes to influencing employees' health and wellbeing beyond the scope of occupational health and safety, a multi-faceted approach is warranted, involving education about what workplace health and wellbeing encapsulate.

EAPs should provide a comprehensive range of wellness services to employees, including, inter alia, traditional counselling, education and support services. Kunte[144] indicated that the offering should comprise a combination of educational, organisational and environmental activities designed to support any behaviours that are conducive to advancing the health of an organisation's employees and their families. These offerings should include lifestyle management programmes; health and wellness education services; peer education and training with regard to, for example, divorce, substance abuse and infection control; and the monitoring and evaluation of the efficacy of such services. At its core, an EAP should assist employees by referring them to places or institutions where they will receive professional help for specific problems. It is thus crucial to the effective functioning of an EAP for practitioners to have the required information available. An EAP practitioner must be able to assist an employee by providing information on where to go, why, who to see/speak to, how to get there, and what the possible cost implications will be.

A comprehensive and regularly updated database is recommended, as it is critical to the success of any EAP. Such a database should contain at least the names and contact details of the various approved service providers within the geographic region of the department and its employees.

Ideally, more information should be available (e.g. cost implications and transport guidelines) to assist employees in obtaining help as soon as possible. EAPs are thus advised to be both proactive and reactive in their approaches to employee assistance.[145]

EAP MODELS OF SERVICE DELIVERY

Research and practice in this field have revealed that EAPs operate under the internal, external, consortium or affiliate models.[146] Joseph and Walker[147] supported the notion that sources of service delivery can comprise internal specialists or employees, external/third-party organisations, or a combination of these.

Internal model

The internal model refers to an in-house EAP, where both diagnosis and treatment services are provided within the institution. In accordance with this model, EAP practitioners are located within the organisation, even though in some instances their offices are located away from the organisation. Rajin[148] noted that with this type of model, the employer maintains a full service facility and employs EAP practitioners on a full-time basis. This implies that the organisation employs the entire employee assistance team and organises their functions into components of a unit. An EAP manager is held accountable for supervising the team, developing EAP policies and frameworks, as well as designing procedures to follow in the implementation of policies.[149]

The EAPA-SA[150] suggested that organisations develop an in-house model for the following reasons and/or purposes:

- Executives themselves are unfamiliar with mental health treatment.
- Employers hire professionals to ensure that an expert deals with employees' problems.
- Organisations wish to show their humanitarian concern for their employees.
- The in-house model is a subcomponent of human resources management, and functions independently.

The internal model provides large companies and public sector organisations with the opportunity to appoint an individual (or a team) who is currently employed within the organisation to render EAP services.[151] With such an in-house service delivery system, the organisation creates an EAP policy, all operations of the programme are employer controlled, members of the EAP team are all employees of the organisation, and the system is more cost effective.[152]

There are several benefits to adopting an internal model for managing EAPs:[153]

- An internal service provides easy access for employees during office hours and this availability encourages utilisation.

- An internal practitioner has greater access to and more readily understands the employees and the culture of the organisation.
- Internal practitioners possess a better knowledge and understanding of the organisation than external vendors do, and as a result a high-quality service designed for a specific organisation may be delivered.
- There is general agreement between managers that in-house EAPs are less costly than external models, and that managers are able to directly use internal control measures.
- More employees who require assistance can easily be identified and referred for appropriate interventions by supervisors.
- In-house models give managers not only direct control of the programme, but ensure that the goals and objectives for which these programmes are institutionalised are understood by the EAP practitioners. The practitioners are also more empathetic towards employees than practitioners who do not possess any knowledge of the organisation or institution.
- In-house EAPs provide employees with a sense of security, because they are not given a quick diagnosis and sent to an outside source.

Despite the numerous benefits outlined above, this model has limitations. According to Rakepa,[154] these include the following:

- Where the service is readily available within close proximity, employees become suspicious of confidentiality and this may render the programme more susceptible to manipulation by management.
- Proximity may be associated with a lack of confidentiality, as information about personal or work-related issues interfering with the individual performance of employees may be used to their disadvantage in terms of their career path.

The in-house model, also called an internal programme, is presented by in-house professionals who are in the employ of the organisation.[155] From the preceding definitions it is evident that an in-house model offers in-company services, with staff members running the programme, which provides a direct link between the EAP and the employee's workplace.

External model

An external or out-of-house model involves a contractual agreement with external EAP service providers either at the facility of the service provider or at a facility provided by the employer. Berridge and Cooper[156] indicated that with an external model, the organisation does not determine the EAP policy – service providers are contracted from outside the organisation and the system is thus more costly. Joseph and Walker[157] stated that globally, as organisations secure

EAPs through tenders, there is great pressure for such programmes to offer whatever their client organisations require or request.

In terms of this model, the organisation is expected to liaise with outside contractors to provide both employee assistance staff and services. This process requires organisations to evaluate proposals from various EAP providers, based on varying internally derived criteria rather than external benchmarks of best practice.[158] For this reason, criteria are generally determined by the organisational strategy, needs, goals and resources, with EAP costings being a major factor to take into account.

The benefits of an external EAP model are the following:[159]

- Improved accountability, decreased legal liability, and ease of start-up and implementation.
- Confidentiality is often maintained, more so than when an in-house EAP model is used.

The external model enables companies, organisations and departments to contract service providers to provide EAP services. These service providers vary from small to large companies, and are known to cater to the needs of those requiring EAP services.[160] This implies that the contractual agreement between the employer and service provider must detail all the specifications regarding how the EAP service should be rendered to employees.

Rakepa[161] presented the following as limitations of the external model:

- External vendors may have limited knowledge about the organisation, which can be detrimental as it will slow intervention processes.
- Having in-depth knowledge about the organisational culture and the demands made upon the employee by the work environment will better equip the EAP practitioner to establish the causes of problems.
- The use of this model usually requires employees to travel to the office of the contractor or service provider, something that can make them reluctant.

According to Straussner,[162] work organisations or unions enter into a contractual agreement with a self-employed social worker, or with personnel employed by an organisation that offers EAP services. The out-of-house model involves employers contracting external providers to provide employees with services at either the facility of the service provider or at a venue made available by the employer.[163]

Consortium and affiliate model

A consortium model is a procedural intervention, mainly developed by small companies, which aims to bring together resources to create a collaborative programme. Rajin[164] highlighted that with the consortium model, different institutions combine their resources (e.g. finances, personnel and facilities) to develop an EAP.

An EAP affiliate is another type of procedural model, coordinated by organisations, through local service providers. The aim is to offer EAP services to employees and their families in private locations closer to their home or office. Such programmes are normally presented at locations external to all stakeholders involved, and are facilitated by a public service agency or commercial enterprise. The EAP affiliate model represents a mix of professionals, including clinical psychologists, substance abuse counsellors, pastoral counsellors, marriage and family therapists, and mental health nurses.[165]

The advantages of a consortium or affiliate model are the following:[166]

- EAPs are designed, structured and staffed by employers who are members of the consortium or affiliate.
- The cost of offering such services is divided amongst member institutions.
- Smaller institutions or organisations receive a cost benefit for outsourcing employee assistance which they cannot afford on their own.

Limitations in operating the consortium or affiliate models are that they are complex in nature, and there may be challenges with decision-making due to the number of stakeholders involved.

RESOURCE ALLOCATION FOR INITIATING THE PROGRAMME

Organisations can ensure that EAPs are implemented successfully by allocating adequate human and financial resources, and by forming partnerships with other institutions, organisations and individuals, where appropriate, that are able to assist. Several barriers to implementation have, however, been cited, including cost, time constraints, logistical issues and cultural barriers.[167] It is crucial that leadership provide support by appointing authoritative management, and allocate sufficient funding and staff to implement and maintain an EAP. Resource allocation is a sign of management's support in ensuring the realisation and utilisation of EAPs. It is important that management not only communicate their EAP's ideas and visions to employees, but also provide support in terms of the necessary financial or human resources to implement the programme. Bear in mind that organisations differ significantly in terms of the budgets and resources they can set aside for an EAP.

EAP human resources

The following section focuses on the appointment, training and skills of the human resource personnel responsible for implementing EAPs.

Appointment of EAP personnel

In an organisation, the decision to adopt an EAP is often the responsibility of the human resources management function.[167] If employers staff the EAP, they can ensure that their employees have access to experienced, formally trained, professional counsellors who are meticulous about maintaining confidentiality. Allocating trained personnel with the right degree of expertise to fulfil multiple roles in running an EAP will ensure the legitimacy of the programme, engender client satisfaction and deliver customised services that not only add value to the lives of employees, but also enhance overall organisational functioning.[169]

When an EAP is not sufficiently staffed and there is a shortage of practitioners in all fields of specialisation, it implies that employees will not receive assistance as and when they require it – they will have to make an appointment and wait their turn. Grobler and Joubert[170] found that staffing an EAP should be a priority; employers need to address the accessibility, availability and response time of practitioners, and ultimately their service delivery (as was the case with the SAPS employees participating in their study). For them, this entailed the immediate filling of vacant posts and the structuring of services to the SAPS at the provincial and cluster station levels.[171] Rajin[172] suggested that in organisations that are not adequately staffed, EAP practitioners must schedule their consultations in such a manner that they do not overburden themselves. A lack of human resources capacity can limit EAPs in their objective of providing support to individuals and organisations.

At the individual level: the aim of EAPs is to tackle individuals' problems in a developmental and optimal way. They relate to employees as a human resource focussing on the following objectives:[173]

- EAPs relate to employees as individual organisational staff members, not as part of an industrial relations collective.
- They tackle perceived problems as seen through the eyes of an employee.
- Their culture places greater emphasis on problem recognition and resolution, and does so in a positive way through an adaptive mode of behaviour.
- They enhance employee flexibility and trainability by developing awareness of resourceful behaviour, and proposing a range of responses to organisational stresses and challenges.
- EAPs constructively provide a way out of disciplinary problems.
- Practitioners provide positive reinforcement that leads to a modification of employee behaviour.

At the organisational level: top management view the impact of EAPs as follows:[174]

- EAPs represent a new strand in the culture of organisations, which does not apportion blame but recognises the existence of stress and helps employees overcome it.

- They provide stress-coping support to help organisations achieve and maintain high levels of employee performance.
- Where the government fails to intervene and counselling is either expensive or unavailable, EAPs act as an organisation's affirmation of social responsibility.
- They are highly effective when compared to traditional, authoritarian supervisory methods aimed at employee rehabilitation.

Personnel or human resources are essential for implementing EAPs. To this end, a team can include EAP practitioners, managers and administrators who are tasked with:[175]

- formulating EAP policies and strategies;
- advising on the implementation of the EAP;
- assisting EAP service providers to correctly position the EAP within departments, in order to optimise benefits;
- continuously promoting, and raising awareness of, EAPs within departments, in close collaboration with EAP service providers;
- developing action plans in conjunction with all the relevant stakeholders;
- coordinating and maintaining a close working alliance between supervisors, employee representatives, employees and EAP service providers; and
- continuously conducting monitoring and evaluation of EAP implementation, in order to assess whether these policies are still relevant, given the ever-changing environment in which organisations function.

Hanisch et al.[176] confirmed that many factors that positively affect employee mental health are related to the social environment at work, such as the working culture, level of social support, and leadership style.

Training and skills of practitioners

Govender[177] argued that professional leadership from a skilled practitioner who enjoys credibility in the eyes of employees is a critical attribute of a successful EAP. For an EAP team to be able to deliver appropriate and effective services, the members need to be trained and knowledgeable in the appropriate fields, and must have access to resources in areas that are of concern to employees. According to Mogorosi,[178] this includes aspects such as counselling; providing substance abuse, health, financial and legal advocacy services; as well as guiding organisational development and social responsibility.

Depending on the EAP model selected, professionals such as occupational social workers, nurses, psychologists and counsellors can be appointed based on their unique professional training and the skills required for each programme. To retain the services of EAP practitioners their salary structure should be market-related, which will help to reduce the rate at which they terminate their services to the organisation. EAP practitioners are professionals, each with their unique field of specialisation, and should thus be regarded as offering a scarce skill set.[179]

Training can extend to the dissemination of information on the potential benefits of promoting workplace health and wellbeing, and aligning these with perceptions relating to healthy and unhealthy employees. To do this, it may be necessary to contextualise the information provided.[180]An EAP practitioner is expected to have comprehensive knowledge of, and proficiency in, diagnosing and treating alcoholism, expertise in offering marriage and family counselling, and thorough knowledge of general emotional problems, as well as other typical problems such as financial and legal troubles. S/he must be able to conduct basic, unbiased interviews. Appointing skilled practitioners can guarantee the organisation that such individuals have basic skills in the counselling methodologies and case management procedures needed to deliver employee assistance services.

Leadership training is critical because of the specialised roles that managers fulfil in organisations. Being in close contact with employees, managers are in the best position to spot signs of deteriorating mental health early on, and to provide support. Unfortunately, many leaders lack training in managing workplace mental health issues, and thus are ill equipped to support affected individuals adequately.[181]

Funding EAPs

The funding model of an EAP largely depends on the scope of the programme, as well as the costs to the company and the willingness of the organisation to foot the bill. Employers have a role to play in creating healthy work environments. In this section, the costs of, and responsibility for, funding EAPs are discussed.

Costs of EAP

Like any other specialist service, EAPs do not come cheap.[182] Positive management support is an investment in the EAP. Indications are that such programmes are becoming autonomous business units within the organisations they serve. Govender[183] highlighted that EAP professionals in organisations are being given greater financial responsibility in bidding for, managing, and reporting on, their own designated budgets. If it functions optimally, such a programme is a cost-effective people management tool that is able to respond to industry expectations.[184] An EAP must thus be an important employee support service, a financially sound investment, and a vital partner in people management.

Employees are not charged for the services provided; no financial transactions are discussed or entered into with the employee for the kind of services EAPs provide. The costs of implementing EAPs vary with regard to the following:

- The type of counselling expertise provided.
- The unique needs of the organisation.
- The workforce of the organisation.
- The stresses and desired/envisaged responses.

Organisations would perceive the costs of running such programmes as having no ascribable relationship to their individual employees, outside of the fact that the services are available to all of them.[185]

Responsibility of the organisation to provide funds

Funding for the implementation of an EAP, its administration and individual employees' counselling generally rests on the shoulders of the employer. In some countries, however, troubled employees are expected to contribute a small amount towards the services provided by EAP practitioners. Where EAPs are offered free of charge to employees, controls in terms of access, frequency and duration of contact must be in place. Usually, each employee is granted a limit (financial or consultation hours), and when that limit is reached, the EAP coordinator reviews the case and can recommend further consultation (or bring an end to consultations).

A study by Pescud et al.[186] found that when the promotion of workplace health and wellbeing was presented to employers as a way to positively influence employees' lives and financial considerations were set aside, those who had previously expressed "nanny state" concerns unexpectedly became enthusiastic about the introduction of health-promoting initiatives. The issue of insufficient budgets can thus be a key debilitating factor in EAP implementation. For the employee, a lack of access might communicate a lack of leadership commitment and passion for intervention programmes. Organisations that are serious about EAPs tend to ensure that practitioners are satisfied with the available budget. They thus need to make decisions about how much financial and practical responsibility to assume, to advance the health and wellbeing of their employees.[187] They thus need to clearly spell out all related financial matters, which depends on the organisation and its context. Organisations that allocate adequate/sufficient budgets to EAPs have the advantage of consistently being more successful in the provision of such services.

It is crucial that appropriate budgets be allocated to EAP units to ensure that they function effectively. Executive leadership need to assume responsibility for budgets. During the initial stage of EAP implementation, it is recommended that organisations implement pilot projects on a smaller scale, i.e., temporary versions of more comprehensive programmes. This should provide an ideal opportunity to test any programmes and/or events, and to determine the actual costs involved. Small corporates seem to find it difficult to fund EAPs, hence many of them do not feel responsible for their employees' health. This does not mean that they are unconcerned about their employees' mental and physical wellbeing, but rather that their limited resources present a challenge.

An EAP budget should finance the salaries of practitioners, transport-related costs, the renting of office space and the purchase of materials necessary to implement the programme. Rajin[188] indicated that EAP practitioners are often challenged by a shortage of office space, which leaves them no room to conduct consultations. This may be a serious issue because confidentiality is one of the principles of EAPs – any interviews/consultations must be conducted in a safe environment which allows employees to outline their personal problems in confidence. Having sufficient office space is important, because consulting with an employee in an office where colleagues may be present is not ethical. This will affect the implementation of the EAP, because employees experiencing deeply personal problems would be hesitant to consult with practitioners where they can be overheard.

A wide range of EAP strategies can be introduced at little or no cost. This means that further investigation into the potential to move away from a return-on-investment approach is warranted. Employee attitudes and perceptions influence the effectiveness of workplace programmes; Hoque[189] argued that if employees perceive the programme to be good and beneficial, and if their attitudes towards the programme are positive, then ultimately their use of the service offerings will increase. If an EAP is not perceived as a viable and available means of support for staff, it is impossible to assess how effective it will be in improving individual and organisational outcomes.[190]

As part of funding, the most common EAP industry pricing approaches (capitated and utilisation-based) entail that fees are determined (fully or in part) according to the number of employees covered by the programme. Milot[191] suggested that a demonstration of benefit equity in outcomes would show the organisation (as purchaser of such services) that the benefits are distributed evenly among the different groups/subgroups of covered employees using those services – even if the majority of employees do not use EAPs during a typical year. This implies that benefit equity could serve as an important differentiator for providers, and act as an additional indicator of programme quality for purchasers to consider when selecting an EAP, along with overall programme effectiveness, pricing, utilisation rates, the range of services offered, and so forth.[192]

CONCLUSION

This chapter outlined the different models and approaches for initiating and implementing EAPs in an organisation. Any practitioner should consider a combination of these approaches and models in their practice. The suggested combination is the application of an internal/in-house model and an external/out-of-house model, while providing both reactive and proactive services. When planning EAPs, a practitioner should determine the financial and human resources required to initiate diverse interventions. Lastly, it is important to ensure that sufficient resources are available and accessible, since a lack of resources may hamper what would otherwise have been efficient, ethical and professional service delivery.

Chapter 4

IMPLEMENTATION OF AN EAP AT THE INDIVIDUAL, GROUP AND ORGANISATIONAL LEVELS

INTRODUCTION

There are various interventions, strategies and techniques that an EAP manager or practitioner can implement. In this chapter, the focus falls on the diverse ways in which a practitioner can address dysfunctions or maladjustments at an individual, group or organisational level. The scope and context of this chapter focuses on different EAP interventions: counselling, coaching, group work, workshops and life skills development programmes which are applicable at the individual, group and organisational levels, and are all aimed at enhancing and addressing performance issues in the workplace.

EAP STRATEGIES APPLICABLE AT THE INDIVIDUAL, GROUP AND ORGANISATIONAL LEVELS

EAP strategies can serve as proactive, reactive or comprehensive measures during the implementation stage. It is important to remember that these strategies are implemented post-assessment. During an assessment the practitioner and the client (individual employee, group or organisation) take a detailed look at the nature and severity of the problem. This might involve meeting with family members, managers or colleagues (if warranted). Upon completion of the assessment, the practitioner and the client discuss which options appear to be the most realistic in resolving the problem. The client chooses the preferred treatment service and a referral (if necessary) is arranged.

Various strategic interventions can form part of EAPs:

Counselling and therapy

Generally speaking, the need to provide help and support to manage employees' personal, familial, work-related and other concerns that could adversely affect their performance in the workplace has been neglected,[193] hence there is a need to offer them counselling and therapy services. According to Sharf,[194] psychotherapy and counselling are interactions between a therapist/counsellor and one or more clients/patients, involving the provision of services that entail the following:

- The purpose is to help the patient/client with problems that may be related to thinking disorders, emotional suffering or behavioural problems.
- Therapists may use their knowledge of the theory of personality and psychotherapy or counselling to help the patient/client improve his/her functioning.
- The therapist's approach to helping must be legally and ethically approved.

McMahon and Palmer[195] described counselling as a deliberate human activity aimed at helping clients in their psychological journey, without resorting to manipulation. During counselling, problems with emotional content are usually discussed during a face-to-face interview with an employee, with a view to helping him/her cope.[196] EAP counselling, which aims to improve the health of stressed employees, is a cost-effective strategy aimed at reducing employee absenteeism and lowering stress levels. Moreover, counselling operates along clearly defined rules with clear intentions, and involves communication, listening and interpersonal skills. It is considered a short-term problem-solving process intended to help emotionally healthy people who are confronted by temporary challenges and crises in their lives.

Telephonic counselling and information helplines are counselling services that professionals provide on a 24-hour basis, which assist individuals who are experiencing a wide range of personal and/or work-related problems. Individuals can make use of a telephone for assistance when confronted with personal problems such as domestic violence (violence within the family, perhaps as a result of family miscommunication). During a counselling session, the counsellor empathetically shares in the experiences, hopes, fears, doubts, setbacks, joy and sadness of the client. Unlike friendship, counselling is not a sympathetic conversation over a cup of tea; counsellors explicitly and temporarily offer their time, attention and respect to clients. It is essential to note that counselling – be it at an individual or group level – must be voluntary.[197] Similarly, it must be provided by qualified and experienced professionals who are capable of working with a broad range of dysfunctions or maladjustments.

The benefits of counselling include the following:

- It affords clients privacy and confidentiality, with no fear of how others will react to their disclosures.
- It grants clients a close relationship with the counsellor, especially when they have no relationship with those closest to them.
- The client receives the full attention of the counsellor.

- Clients are seen in a therapeutic environment, especially when their problems relate to their relationships with themselves and do not involve others.
- Clients enter a safe arena in which to explore their options, without the influence or interference of others (e.g. spouses or partners).

Counselling (interviewing, guiding and advising) is a structured conversation aimed at improving a client's quality of life in the face of adversity. Employee counselling could focus on issues such as understanding the self, decision-making, goal setting, planning for the future and managing interpersonal problems.[198] Rajin[199] indicated that an effective EAP is based on professional counselling, which requires specific inputs from a supervisor or manager. She noted that:

- the success of the EAP rests on the observational skills of the supervisor;
- supervisors, mainly as a result of their daily interactions with subordinates, are able to identify personal problems that affect job performance negatively; and
- the supervisor can use such interactions to help employees solve their problems by referring them for counselling or treatment long before the problem deteriorates.

In addition to the above, there is evidence that counselling assists individuals and groups to develop a set of values that makes life more meaningful, to learn social behaviour that improves the quality of human relationships, and to try to resolve any dysfunctions that hinder them from leading more satisfying lives. Counselling must, however, be implemented ethically. If employees feel that the service/service providers are not trustworthy or maintaining confidentiality they will not participate wholeheartedly, nor will they gain maximum benefit from such a programme.[200]

Therapy is an intervention that can be used for behaviour modification and cognitive restructuring in clients. Short-term or brief therapy describes a group of therapeutic interventions aimed at solving the client's problem within the shortest amount of time possible.[201] Rakepa[202] indicated that therapeutic services are intended to treat mental and psychological problems that impede the full functioning of individuals. For this reason, such interventions are mainly provided by practitioners with professional expertise in a broad area.

Different theories can be used for therapy and counselling, depending on a practitioner's preferences and skill set. Sharf[203] identified various types of theories which are applicable in psychotherapy and counselling.

Table 4.1: Psychotherapy and counselling theories

Theory	Description
Psychoanalysis	Sigmund Freud stressed the importance of inborn drives (particularly sexual) in determining later personality development. Others who followed him emphasized the importance of adaptation to the environment, early relationships between child and mother, and developmental changes in being absorbed with oneself at the expense of meaningful relationships with others. All of these views of development make use of Freud's concepts of unconscious processes (portions of mental functioning that we are not aware of) and, in general, his structure of personality (ego, id, superego). Traditional psychoanalytic methods require several years of treatment. Because of this, moderate-length and brief therapy methods that use more direct, rather than indirect, techniques have been developed. New writings continue to explore the importance of childhood development on later personality as well as new uses of the therapist's relationship.
Jungian Analysis and Therapy	More than any other theorist, Jung placed great emphasis on the role of unconscious processes in human behaviour. Jungians are particularly interested in dreams, fantasies, and other material that reflects unconscious processes. They are also interested in symbols of universal patterns that are reflected in the unconscious processes of people from all cultures. Therapy focuses on the analysis of unconscious processes so that patients can better integrate unconscious processes into conscious awareness.
Adlerian Therapy	Alfred Adler believed that the personality of individuals was formed in their early years as a result of relationships within the family. He emphasized the importance of individuals' contributions to their community and to society. Adlerians are interested in the ways that individuals approach living and family relationships. The Adlerian approach to therapy is practical, helping individuals to change dysfunctional beliefs and encouraging them to take new steps to change their lives. An emphasis on teaching and educating individuals about dealing with interpersonal problems is another characteristic of Adlerian therapy.

Theory	Description
Existential Therapy	A philosophical approach to people and problems relating to being human or existing, existential psychotherapy deals with life themes rather than techniques. Such themes include living and dying, freedom, responsibility to self and others, finding meaning in life, and dealing with a sense of meaninglessness. Becoming aware of oneself and developing the ability to look beyond immediate problems and daily events to deal with existential themes are goals of therapy, along with developing honest and intimate relationships with others. Although some techniques have been developed, the emphasis is on issues and themes, not method.
Person-centred Therapy	In his therapeutic work, Carl Rogers emphasized understanding and caring for the client, as opposed to diagnosis, advice, or persuasion. Characteristic of Rogers's approach to therapy are therapeutic genuineness, through verbal and nonverbal behaviour, and unconditionally accepting clients for who they are. Person-centred therapists are concerned about understanding the client's experience and communicating their understanding to the client so that an atmosphere of trust can be developed that fosters change on the part of the client. Clients are given responsibility for making positive changes in their lives.
Gestalt Therapy	Developed by Fritz Perls, gestalt therapy helps the individual to become more aware of self and others. Emphasis is on both bodily and psychological awareness. Therapeutic approaches deal with being responsible for oneself and attuned to one's language, nonverbal behaviours, emotional feelings, and conflicts within oneself and with others. Therapeutic techniques include the development of creative experiments and exercises to facilitate self-awareness.
Behaviour Therapy	Based on scientific principles of behaviour, such as classical and operant conditioning, as well as observational learning, behaviour therapy applies principles of learning such as reinforcement, extinction, shaping of behaviour, and modelling to help a wide variety of clients with different problems. Emphasis is on precision and detail in evaluating psychological concerns and then assigning treatment methods that may include relaxation, exposure to a feared object, copying a behaviour, or role playing. Its many techniques include those that change observable behaviour as well as those that deal with thought processes.

Theory	Description
Rational Emotive Behavior Therapy	Developed by Albert Ellis, rational emotive behavior therapy (REBT) focuses on irrational beliefs that individuals develop that lead to problems related to emotions (for example, fears and anxieties) and to behaviors (such as avoiding social interactions or giving speeches). Although REBT uses a wide variety of techniques, the most common method is to dispute irrational beliefs and to teach clients to challenge their own irrational beliefs so that they can reduce anxiety and develop a full range of ways to interact with others.
Cognitive Therapy	Belief systems and thinking are seen as important in determining and affecting behavior and feelings. Aaron Beck developed an approach that helps individuals understand their own maladaptive thinking and how it may affect their feelings and actions. Cognitive therapists use a structured method to help their clients understand their own belief systems. By asking clients to record dysfunctional thoughts and using questionnaires to determine maladaptive thinking, cognitive therapists are then able to make use of a wide variety of techniques to change beliefs that interfere with successful functioning. They also make use of affective and behavioral strategies.
Reality Therapy	Reality therapists assume that individuals are responsible for their own lives and for taking control over what they do, feel, and think. Developed by William Glasser, reality therapy uses a specific process to change behaviour. A relationship is developed with clients so that they will commit to the therapeutic process. Emphasis is on changing behaviors that will lead to modifications in thinking and feeling. Making plans and sticking to them to bring about change while taking responsibility for oneself are important aspects of reality therapy.
Constructivist Therapy	Constructivist therapists see their clients as theorists and try to understand their clients' views or the important constructs that clients use to understand their problems. Three types of constructivist theories are discussed: solution-focused, personal construct theory, and narrative. Solution-focused therapy centres on finding solutions to problems by looking at what has worked in the past and what is working now, as well as using active techniques to make therapeutic progress.

Theory	Description
Constructivist Therapyn (continued)	Personal construct theory examines clients' lives as stories and helps to change the story. Narrative therapies also view clients' problems as stories but seek to externalize the problem, unlike personal construct theory. Frequently, they help clients re-author or change stories, thus finding a new ending for the story that leads to a solution to the problem.
Feminist Therapy	Rather than focusing only on the individual's psychological problems, feminist therapists emphasize the role of politics and society in creating problems for individuals. Particularly, they are concerned about gender and cultural roles and power differences between men and women and people from diverse cultural backgrounds. They have examined different ways that gender and culture affect development throughout the life span (including social and sexual development, child-raising practices, and work roles). Differences in moral decision-making, relating to others, and roles in abuse and violence are issues of feminist therapists. By combining feminist therapy with other theories, feminist therapists take a sociological as well as a psychological view that focuses not only on gender but also on multicultural issues. Among the techniques they use are those that help individuals address gender and power inequalities, not only by changing client behaviour but also by changing societal groups or institutions.
Family Therapy	Whereas many theories focus on the problems of individuals, family therapists attend to interactions between family members and may view the entire family as a single unit or system. Treatment is designed to bring about change in functioning within the family rather than within a single individual. Several different approaches to family therapy have been developed. Some focus on the impact of the parents' own families, others on how family members relate to each other in the therapy hour, and yet others on changing symptoms. Some family systems therapists request that all the family members be available for therapy, whereas others may deal with parents or certain members only.

Theory	Description
Other Psychotherapy Theories	Asian therapies often emphasize quiet reflection and personal responsibility to others. Body therapies work with the interaction between psychological and physiological functioning. Interpersonal therapy is a very specific treatment for depression based on a review of research. Psychodrama is an active system in which clients, along with group and audience members, play out roles related to their problems while therapists take responsibility for directing the activities. Creative arts therapies include art, dance movement, drama, and music to encourage expressive action and therapeutic change. Any of these therapies may be used with other therapeutic approaches.

Source: Sharf (2012:6–7)

Therapy is applied to change weak and scattered thoughts, using strong and concentrated techniques. Its purpose is to use interaction to motivate behaviour change and develop an individual development plan, which must maximise strengths and minimise weaknesses. Nagesar[204] indicated that therapy can only be successful if the client is able to acknowledge that there is a problem and that a solution is being sought. Therapy helps clients to develop awareness of their problems in order to assist them to make choices, determine their purpose of existence and become self-sufficient.

Behaviour modification or cognitive restructuring is only effective when clients are aware of their problems, are determined to expend effort to address these, and are in touch with their current reality. Govender[205] believed that short-term therapy is an important approach for EAPs, since it helps practitioners to provide a cost-effective, time-limited therapy which benefits both employers and employees. This strategic intervention is the most appropriate for EAPs, since the bottom line in the world of work is that time is money, thus they have to add value to the organisation, group and/or individual client.

The process of therapy entails the following:[206]

- Working with clients who have a significant level of psychopathology or emotional distress, so as to arrive at an analysis of the problem.
- Focusing on resolving past traumas that affect personality development.
- Changing personality structures.
- Attempting to relieve psychic pain, anxiety or depression.
- Offering specific expertise in the area of need.

Despite their differences, these theories can be integrated by combining two or more theories. Such integration occurs when theories are used in different ways to understand client problems; using a wide variety of techniques can help clients effect changes in their lives.[207]

Coaching

Coaching occurs in one-on-one conversations that involve listening, questioning and constructive feedback. It has been embraced in organisations as an important technique that addresses employee performance, improves productivity and even elevates profits.[208] The central function of coaching is to facilitate personal and professional change and development. Coaches draw on their vast experience to motivate, facilitate and guide employees towards making positive changes in response to work dysfunctions. A client and a coach can enter into a one-on-one coaching relationship in order to improve professional performance and increase the client's level of personal life satisfaction. Coaching as an EAP intervention thus involves a paradigm shift which works towards instilling positive organisational behaviour.[209]

Boyce, Jackson and Neal[210] highlighted three key processes in a coaching relationship:

- Rapport: this involves minimising differences between the client and the coach, while building on similarities. It entails arriving at a mutual understanding. Rapport allows both parties to appreciate, recognise and respect each other. A strong rapport increases the client's level of self-disclosure, his/her satisfaction and the chances of an effective treatment outcome.
- Trust: this involves the client's confidence, willingness to open up, honesty and vulnerability during the coaching process. Trust establishes a safe environment that allows the coach to be more supportive, non-judgemental and challenging, while supporting the client's personal growth and sense of satisfaction. It is through trust and confidentiality that both the client and coach can develop an open and honest dialogue.
- Commitment: this refers to a dedication to perform tasks and fulfil responsibilities. Both the client and coach are considered committed when they adhere to scheduled appointments, are accessible, prepare for meetings and persevere despite setbacks.

Three types of coaching can be applied in EAPs: one-on-one, group and systems coaching. Nagesar[211] described these categories as follows:

- One-on-one coaching involves working with individuals on a person-to-person basis.
- Group coaching is conducted with several people who have a shared interest.
- Systems coaching refers to working with or within a system, for example an organisation or institution.

Coaching at an organisational level implies that the EAP practitioner should be positioned as a strategic partner who provides management consultation in order to help explain relevant aspects of human behaviour and find solutions to human resource issues. Organisational assistance is a special responsibility the EAP practitioner has towards the organisation as a client – it is an extension of his/her client service. The process followed by professional coaches entails the following:[212]

- A collaborative, egalitarian (based on the principle of equality) relationship.
- A focus on constructive solutions.
- A collaborative, goal-setting process.
- Expertise in facilitating learning.
- Systematic processes which are aimed at expediting goal attainment.
- Self-directed learning and personal growth for sustained change.

Organisational assistance in the form of coaching involves:

- advocacy in relation to specific client needs, interventions which are designed to modify the attitudes/behaviours of significant others in the workplace who aggravate an employee's dysfunction, or mediating when interpersonal problems arise;
- becoming a confidential source of information and offering guidance to those who are overwhelmed or perplexed by incomprehensible employee behaviour;
- addressing any work-related crises affecting a particular group that may have a detrimental impact on the overall performance of the work unit;
- influencing organisational culture by intervening to effect changes in attitudes and beliefs, to create a more conducive frame of mind which promotes the welfare of both the organisation and the individual employee (e.g. through informational or educational efforts); and
- using specialised EAP knowledge, expertise and experience to guide decision-making processes and the implementation of policies, especially those pertaining to the health and welfare of employees (adapted from Govender[213]).

Group work

Group work is an EAP strategy that offers employees an opportunity to realise that they are not the only ones facing certain problems,[214] which provides them with an environment in which they can feel free to express their thoughts, emotions and feelings.[215] The EAPA[216] indicates that practitioners can also use core technologies to further assist employees who experience similar problems in a group, so that colleagues may learn from one another how best to confront their challenges and become effective in the workplace.

Nagesar[217] indicated that group work can take the form of therapy, counselling or coaching, which is conducted with several employees who have a shared concern or problem. Groups are useful in that they allow members to share information, debate around issues and solve problems together. They are most effective when facilitators possess strong group work skills and are flexible in their use of session time. Group work can also serve as a prevention programme in the workplace, by establishing systematic patterns of activities to bring about change in the group, rather than in an individual employee.

Sharf indicated that group therapy has the advantage of being more efficient than individual therapy because it serves more people at the same time, while offering certain benefits that individual therapy does not. The following are the benefits of group work or therapy:[218]

- When compared with individual therapy, participants in group therapy can learn effective social skills and try out new styles of relating to other members of the group.
- Group members are often peers and thus represent (in some ways) a microcosm of the society clients deal with daily.
- Because groups exist to help members with a variety of problems, group members can offer support to one another, to explore and work on important problems.
- Groups help individuals become more caring and sensitive to the needs and problems of others.
- Although most groups are therapeutic in nature, focusing on the development of interpersonal skills or psychological problems, others have a more educational function, i.e., teaching clients skills that may be useful in their lives.

Group work is based on allowing employees to work through several group stages. Practitioners (as group leaders) should be able to manage these phases:[219]

- Initial phase: the role of the leader at this stage is to model, provide structure, delegate responsibility, establish group norms, foster group cohesion, help group members derive the most from the group experience, and identify goals for the programme. This stage is compared to those of exploration and orientation during infancy. Members are concerned about inclusion and identity, as well as establishing trust.
- Transition phase: this phase is characterised by anxiety, defensiveness and resistance, a struggle for control, conflict and challenges to the group. The group leader should deal with problem behaviour and difficult members by demonstrating the value of silence; encouraging participation; denouncing monopolistic behaviour; appreciating storytelling, questioning and the giving of advice; avoiding band-aiding; quelling hostile, dependent, or seductive behaviour; and encouraging socialising, intellectualising and emotionalising of the process.

- Working phase: during this stage the group focuses on dealing with issues. Therapeutic factors that operate in groups include self-disclosure, confrontation, feedback, cohesion, hope, willingness to risk and trust, empathy and caring, power, catharsis, cognitive restricting, commitment to change, freedom to experiment, and humour.
- Termination phase: this is characterised by group members' behaviours and feelings of denial, regression, reactivation, flight, contingency plans, reviewing, reduced activity, anger, despair, anxiety and grief. As a leader, the practitioner should be able to deal with group feelings and unfinished business; s/he should review the group experience, take the learning further, and give and receive feedback.

Confidentiality is an important matter in group work and should be discussed with members at the beginning of the group session. Group leaders (especially practitioners) are, however, bound by the ethics and legalities of their profession, and are prevented from disclosing information that has serious implications for people's health and safety. For group members to share their concerns and feelings during a group session, group facilitators must develop and maintain trust.

Workshops, seminars and life skills development

Employee workshops are amongst the EAP intervention strategies arranged by organisations to enhance the psychological wellbeing and health of staff, with a view to ensuring employee retention and increasing organisational revenue.[220] Workshops are normally introduced according to the level of employees' educational level. Health management workshops, for instance, focus on employees' total physical and mental condition. They are, amongst others, aimed at reducing employees' stress levels by stimulating both the body and the brain.

In today's workforce, multiple skills are needed: thinking, personal, resource allocation, interpersonal, organisational and leadership skills all serve to enhance productivity and make employment more meaningful.[221] Employee development is an important tool in maintaining and developing the capabilities of both the employee and the organisation.[222] Life skills development programmes are more likely to develop employee confidence and employability, by focusing on interpersonal skills which can improve employee relationships. This can be done via seminars dealing with budgeting, communication, preventing harassment or team building, for example. A study conducted at the Department of Water Affairs and Forestry[223] found that most participants wished to participate in the following education programmes:

- Personal financial management (68%).
- HIV/Aids (51%).
- Marriage, family and child-related issues (45%).
- Transfer issues (43%).

Swanepoel,[224] who conducted research into the Cape Medical Plan, found that managers and employees expressed training needs for personal as well as work-related problems. These included:

- stress management;
- relationship building;
- communication skills;
- conflict management;
- assertiveness;
- management of depression; and
- marriage and family support.

Seminars and workshops provide the necessary skills to help employees become more competent for jobs within their organisations, while conditions under which employees believe they are being valued and cared for by their organisation can be created through skills development opportunities. Such employees take their cues from their organisations with regard to development, which leads to high levels of organisational commitment and greater job satisfaction.

Crisis management and trauma debriefing

Crisis management is a strategy aimed at dealing with critical incidents, i.e., events with the potential to overwhelm an employee's usual coping mechanisms. Such events cause psychological distress and often impair normal adaptive functioning. Types of critical incidents include a line-of-duty death; a suicide or homicide; mass casualties; hostage situations; natural disasters resulting in severe injury/death or destruction; and workplace violence in which someone's life is threatened.[225]

Employees who have encountered critical incidents tend to become less productive; they are frequently absent from work and are at greater risk of causing (or being involved in) accidents. For these reasons, critical incidents cause significant disruptions throughout an organisation and evoke a wide range of negative cognitive, behavioural and emotional responses. A critical incident can thus be defined as any situation facing employees which causes them to experience a strong emotional reaction that can potentially interfere with their ability to function effectively.

A trauma is a powerful and overwhelming event that lies outside the range of usual human experience. Trauma debriefing is a technique that can be used to manage a crisis in an organisation and to help employees recover from critical incidents. Govender[226] explained that debriefings are structured sessions, conducted with larger groups, within 24–72 hours after an incident. They involve confidential discussions about the trauma, which affords participants an opportunity to put the traumatic experiences into perspective and accelerate their recovery period.

Rakepa[227] indicated that when used effectively for psychological debriefing, trauma debriefing empowers individuals and groups who have suffered traumatic experiences, as it prevents employees from misinterpreting their own personal reactions and being vulnerable to post-traumatic stress disorder.

The following processes in crisis/incident management have been identified:[228]

- Pre-incident education: information about stress resilience.
- Supportive contacts: providing support to an individual on a one-on-one basis.
- Defusing: a group technique to provide closure.
- Debriefing: a group process model to mitigate acute symptoms.
- Crisis management briefings (CMSes): provide information and do rumour control.
- Demobilisation: ongoing structured, emotional support.
- Follow-up/referrals: link affected people and give feedback.

The EAP practitioner's role in a traumatic or critical incident situation is to assist victims to cope with the event immediately after it occurred. Defusing, if held within one to four hours of a traumatic event, helps to stabilise employees and allows them re-entry into the trauma situation or a return home to recuperate following a reduction in the levels of debilitating stress.[229]

WELLNESS PROGRAMMES AS A STRATEGY

Another EAP strategic intervention is the implementation of a wellness programme. Kunte[230] stated that organisations are internationally recognised as appropriate settings for health promotion if they offer wellness programmes as part of their human resource strategies. Wellness programmes can be described as long-term organisational activities designed to promote the adoption of organisational practices and personal behaviours which are conducive to maintaining or improving employees' physiological and mental wellbeing.[231] Current trends in the field regard wellness centres as a critical component of the EAP scope of practice. It is through wellness initiatives that an organisation can move beyond remedying dysfunctions to promote an environment of wellbeing.

Wellness encompasses various conscious and responsible actions aimed at balancing the integrated dimensions of an individual's existence (physical, emotional, intellectual, spiritual, occupational and social). The aim is to achieve the highest potential for personal health and wellbeing, thus wellness programmes should comprise a combination of educational, organisational and environmental activities designed to support health-conscious behaviour amongst not only employees, but also their families.[232]

The purpose of wellness programmes and centres is to:

- support employees in balancing the demands of their work and personal lives;
- offer consultation services to corporations on how to provide a family-friendly, supportive environment aimed at increasing creativity and productivity in the workplace;
- maximise the individual's health and wellbeing, to lower healthcare costs and increase workforce productivity; and
- improve employees' welfare benefits and morale, in order to enhance the corporate image of the organisation.

Principles and benefits of wellness programmes

Wellness programmes and centres work on the assumption of positive psychology that employee wellbeing can be enhanced by focusing on people's strengths, rather than on those limitations that cause dysfunctions. The objective of positive psychology theory is to highlight human beings' strengths and optimal functioning, not their weaknesses and malfunctioning.[233]

According to Nagesar,[234] four key principles should be kept in mind when establishing a wellness centre or programme in an organisation:

- The first principle is to integrate the wellness programme into the coordinated health programme.
- The second principle is to tailor the programme to the health needs of employees.
- The third principle is to encourage stakeholders to start small and build on a solid foundation.
- The fourth principle is to gather support from a cross-section of the organisation as a community.

Wellness in the workplace can be viewed as a broad concept comprising personal satisfaction, work–life satisfaction, and general health (which is a combination of mental/psychological and physical/physiological health).[235] Wellness programmes and centres seem to have far-reaching benefits for employees as well as for organisations, in respect of achieving their strategic objectives (if implemented appropriately).

The benefits of wellness programmes are:[236]

- reduced costs associated with employee health plans and employee compensation;
- reduced cost of replacing valued employees who are lost to injury or illness;
- increased employee retention by providing an additional benefit in the form of EAPs; and
- satisfying humanitarian concerns for employees' wellbeing.

Development and implementation of wellness programmes

Pescud et al.[237] indicated that motivations for wellness programmes are based on the definition of a healthy workplace as one that maximises the integration of employees' goals for wellbeing, and organisational objectives for profitability and productivity. Relaxation, balance, flexibility and focus are four key components of such programmes, while wellness programmes and centres use resilience training to improve wellness. To a large extent, a programme's effectiveness depends on an individual's self-awareness and self-management.

Employee wellness practices in organisations that have inculcated a healthy workplace culture through health interventions have several elements in common. Successful programmes focus on: (1) organisational commitment; (2) incentives for employees to participate; (3) effective screening and triage; (4) state-of-the-art theory and evidence-based interventions; (5) effective implementation; and (6) ongoing programme evaluation.[238]

Nagesar[239] identified nine steps to establishing a wellness programme in the context of an EAP:

Step 1: Obtain administrative support.

Step 2: Identify resources.

Step 3: Identify a leader.

Step 4: Organise a committee.

Step 5: Gather and analyse data.

Step 6: Develop a plan.

Step 7: Implement the plan.

Step 8: Evaluate and adapt the programme.

Step 9: Sustain the programme.

According to Rakepa,[240] wellness programmes include various health promotion initiatives:

- Complex care management refers to the coordination of types of service used by employees. These services include medical care, disability programmes, workers' compensation programmes, as well as absenteeism and occupational safety programmes. Complex care management is a method of helping employers to consider the impact and consequence of illnesses experienced by their employees.
- Chronic disease management: a chronic disease is an illness that persists for a long time, therefore organisations must have systems in place to deal with such occurrences. They

must develop programmes for effective communication, encourage knowledge of disease management, change attitudes and behaviours, reduce stigma and discrimination, as well as care and support vulnerable employees.

- Healthcare consumer education: consumers in this context are viewed as users of services in the workplace, i.e., employees. Healthcare consumer education is a preventative measure aimed at sensitising employees with regard to health-related issues, and entails anticipating health issues that require intervention before they reach crisis levels.
- Nurse line for enquiries and health education: this occurs when the organisation has outsourced some of its services for disease management to vendors who offer, amongst other services, a nurse line for enquiries and health education. Qualified nurses employed by the vendor telephonically advise employees on health-related matters.

Organisations that have wellness centres mostly provide gym facilities, restaurants that promote healthy eating, health screening, health risk appraisals, educational activities, behaviour change programmes and high-risk interventions. Management's responsibility regarding wellness programmes is clearly important (and often legislated), yet the lines are somewhat blurred and discretionary in relation to activities covered under the broader topic of health and wellbeing.[241] When management aligns health interventions with specific health concerns, it can go a long way in deciding the effectiveness of such programmes.[242]

Other initiatives of wellness programmes are childcare and elderly care services, flexible work arrangements and family participation.[242] Most organisations find it difficult to sustain wellness centres due to financial constraints, as managers tend to regard short-term survival as more important than the long-term returns flowing from wellness programmes[244] – after all, the majority of organisations are concerned with a need to contain rising healthcare costs. Another area that influences the wellness of employees, but is often considered separately from health promotion initiatives, is occupational health and safety (OHS) or health protection. According to Pescud et al.,[245] OHS encompasses efforts aimed at preventing injury or illness due to workplace-specific exposure, by conducting safety training, environmental modification, and the provision and use of personal protective equipment.

A study in the South African mining sector, which sought to develop and implement a safety leadership-coaching programme and evaluate the impact thereof on safety leadership, found the following:[246]

- The ratings of safety leadership were generally higher post-assessment than pre-assessment.
- Significant improvements were reported on three dimensions of safety leadership, namely accountability, collaboration, and feedback and recognition.

Some of the interesting results of this study were that:

- coaching was the best management development intervention for middle managers (rather than senior management). The management levels' post-test ratings were on average 0.43 points higher than their pre-test ratings, i.e., an average increase of 13% between pre- and post-test results, which translated into statistically significant improvements on six of the eight safety leadership dimensions;
- coaching had the greatest impact on the interpersonal and communication aspects linked to collaborative or participative behaviours. This was evident in that the dimension of feedback and recognition received the lowest pre-test ratings but was rated significantly higher on the post-test by seven of the 16 groups;
- performance improvement and behavioural changes after coaching are observable to others;
- coaching had a positive impact on managers' attitudes towards safety, as was evident after they had completed the programme; and
- the aspect of the coaching programme that contributed most to changing managers' attitudes toward safety was an increase in their legal knowledge and their subsequent increased awareness of their legal responsibilities in terms of occupational health and safety (see Esterhuizen, 2014).

The results of this study indicate the value of a coaching programme in improving the occupational health of an organisation.

CONCLUSION

This chapter is critical for helping EAP practitioners understand the various strategies and theories available to them. Knowing the advantages and disadvantages of counselling, therapy, trauma debriefing, crisis management, group work and life skills development should enable practitioners to make informed decisions in their practices. Wellness programmes have received recognition in the field of EAP as strategic interventions, and they may be considered once an organisation's needs have been taken into account.

Chapter 5

STAKEHOLDER MANAGEMENT AND THE MARKETING OF AN EAP

INTRODUCTION

Practitioners and managers can ensure the effective and successful implementation of an EAP through the active participation of all relevant stakeholders. This chapter describes the process of identifying all the internal and external stakeholders who engage with the organisation, before providing guidelines on how to formulate an internal EAP marketing plan targeted at all employees.

STAKEHOLDER ENGAGEMENT IN EAPs

In South African workplaces, EAPs are inadequately understood and used.[247] This has resulted in a lack of sensitivity to employees' work-related (and unrelated) problems, which include stress. For this reason it is the responsibility of both management and EAP practitioners to change the status quo and promote the use of such programmes to all the relevant stakeholders.

Definition and types of stakeholders

A stakeholder is someone or some entity with a stake in a company;[248] it refers to anyone with a vested interest in an organisation, irrespective of whether the organisation has the same interest in them. Ledimo[249] stated that the term "stakeholder" refers to any person(s), group(s) or organisation(s) which the leaders, managers and employees of an organisation should take into account. In other words, stakeholders are groups or individuals who affect or are affected by the achievements and performance of an organisation. Since their legitimacy, contributions and roles are vital for the survival and success of an organisation, stakeholders might include shareholders, managers, customers, employees, suppliers and even the community.

Caroll[250] differentiated between primary and secondary stakeholders as per the below:

- Primary or internal stakeholders: these stakeholders – who have a direct, contractual relationship with the organisation – can include employees, the board of directors, managers, investors, senior management, head office, consumers, shareholders, competitors and suppliers. Internal stakeholders are individuals or parties who have a direct impact in or on the organisation.

- Secondary or external stakeholders: such stakeholders may be impacted by the actions of the organisation, despite not being contractually connected to it. Examples include suppliers, creditors, clients, intermediaries, competitors, society, government, environmental groups, the community, local government, non-governmental organisations (NGOs), family members and labour unions. External stakeholders are individuals or parties who have an indirect impact in or on the organisation.

Information about available services can be disseminated by other departments in an organisation – which are also stakeholders – such as human resources and health/medical divisions (e.g. clinics) which are in constant contact with employees.[251] To summarise: stakeholders are any groups that have a relationship with an organisation; they have an interest in an organisation's operations and performance, because of their relationship with the organisation.[252]

Stakeholder engagement

Stakeholder engagement refers to endeavours on the part of an organisation to involve strategic stakeholders in the decision-making process.[253] Engagement is aimed at strengthening the internal corporate image by encouraging employees to participate in organisational activities. Thus, stakeholder engagement is a means of providing employees access to decision-making processes and encouraging them to actively take part in the activities of an organisation. This can be achieved through the three elements of stakeholder engagement, which infer that core issues affecting both management and general employees should be made known to, understood, and addressed by all parties concerned.

Stakeholder theory emphasises that the relationship between management and general employees should be orientated towards achieving mutually beneficial objectives that are based on high ethical and moral standards, rather than self-interest. Table 5.1 illustrates the theoretical statements pertaining to both stakeholder theory and stakeholder engagement principles.

Table 5.1: Stakeholder theory and stakeholder engagement principles

Principles	Statements
Stakeholder theory	• The organisation has high ethical and moral standards. • General employees' ethical and moral standards are congruent with those of management. • The relationship between general employees and management is mutually beneficial. • Management and general employees have shared objectives in realising the success of the organisation.

Principles	Statements
Stakeholder engagement principles	• Materiality: both management and general employees are aware of one another's most prominent concerns. Materiality emphasises that the most relevant issues facing an organisation and its stakeholders should be known. • Completeness: management understands general employees' concerns related to their views, needs and performance expectations. Completeness stresses that the views, needs and performance expectations (material issues) of stakeholders should be understood by the organisation. • Responsiveness: both management and general employees' concerns should be actively addressed, where general employees are involved in resolving the organisational concerns raised by management. Responsiveness stipulates that there should be reasonable responses (relating to decisions, actions, performance and communication) to all stakeholders, when addressing material issues.

Source: Slabbert (2015)

Stakeholders who feel ignored and misunderstood are inclined to place limits on the implementation of organisational objectives.[254] The following forms of resistance strategies indicate the ways in which stakeholders put pressure on, or resist, such processes:[255]

- Acquiescence resistance can take alternative forms, including habit, imitation and compliance.
- Compromise resistance includes balancing, pacifying and bargaining with the organisation.
- Avoidance resistance is when stakeholders conceal their nonconformity, buffer or defend themselves using organisational rules and expectations.
- Defiance resistance, as an active form of resistance to organisational processes, can manifest itself as non-participation, challenge or attack.
- Active manipulation resistance refers to a purposeful or opportunistic attempt to co-opt, influence or control organisational processes.

Resistance may occur during the implementation of an EAP, thus practitioners and managers should have a plan and strategies in place to deal with this eventuality. To this end, Ledimo[256] proposed five stakeholder resistance management strategies:

- Adaptation strategy: this strategy obeys the demands and rules presented by stakeholders.
- Compromising strategy: a strategy used when practitioners negotiate with stakeholders, listen to their claims about the diagnosis process, and offer possibilities and arenas for dialogue.
- Avoidance strategy: in terms of this strategy, practitioners loosen their attachment to stakeholders and their claims, so as to shield themselves. This occurs when managers transfer the responsibility of responding to claims to another actor in the project network.
- Dismissal strategy: this is used when practitioners ignore the presented demands of stakeholders and do not take into account stakeholder-related pressures and their requirements in the execution of the project.
- Influence strategy: this is used when a practitioner embarks on the process of proactively shaping the values and demands of stakeholders. It is implemented when practitioners actively share information and build relationships with all stakeholders.

Unions as critical stakeholders

Unions or organised labour are primary stakeholders in the organisation, as they represent employees.[257] One of several contentions within the EAP field is the conflict between management prerogatives and labour rights with respect to the work environment, and the function of EAPs in mediating between the interests of these two parties.[258] Stakeholders' support and involvement can increase by including union officials in sessions aimed at training managers to use constructive confrontation strategies both fairly and compassionately. Labour union support and involvement can improve the effectiveness of an EAP, but it is common knowledge that not all organisational endeavours will gain the support of all employees and their unions.

Unions should be involved in policy formulation, because when they are side-lined it becomes difficult for them to offer labour support to EAPs. Unions are usually in favour of employers introducing EAPs in the workplace, because one of their primary aims is to represent their members when the latter's wellbeing is affected. Training for union representatives and stewards should be done at least once a year, and should cover a wide range of issues such as substance abuse, family problems, intervention strategies and the referral process.[259]

The effectiveness of an EAP might be increased if labour and management work together informally. Both unions and employees need to participate in these programmes, since the clients/beneficiaries of these programmes are union members.

Rakepa[260] presented the following benefits of engaging unions as key stakeholders:

- When dealing with the initiation of formal disciplinary measures, co-operation between organisations and unions regarding the EAP has yielded positive results (i.e., a better understanding of processes amongst all involved).

- The majority of employee problems can be resolved before disciplinary measures are called for. Once formal disciplinary measures take effect, the union will defend its members.
- Co-operation between management and labour unions is vital to prevent the situation from reaching the point of dispute.
- When unions are involved they will support the programme, as they view it as an additional benefit for their members.

There is a limitation in that when programme aims are rather modest, in most organisations cooperation becomes difficult to achieve and tends to occur at the lower rather than the higher levels.[261] Without union support EAPs may be viewed with suspicion, scepticism and resistance, hence to ensure support, proper consultation processes need to take place among all parties concerned.[262]

Management and leadership as key stakeholders

The engagement of management and leadership in the organisation normally assumes the form of managerial support. Leadership support for EAPs is defined as their involvement in, and promotion of, any activities, policies and practices that encourage the development of a health-promotion climate that integrates this aspect into the organisational strategy.[263] Such support is crucial for ensuring the realisation and utilisation of the programme, and for communicating its vision at different levels of the organisation.[264] It is critical that organisational management endorse EAPs and what they aim to do. As employees' perceptions greatly influence their decisions and behaviour, management must be seen to be driving and contributing to EAPs if employees are to utilise such interventions. Mogorosi[265] indicated that EAP endorsement can be demonstrated by management's vocal and practical approval or promotion of any activities carried out under the auspices of such a programme.

The benefits of having employees witness leadership as being actively involved in developing and maintaining EAPs should not be underestimated. Senior managers exert a strong influence on all aspects of organisational functioning, and gaining the support of top management for an EAP sends out a message that management understands the importance of employee health, and is prepared to devote considerable time and resources to identifying and addressing priority health issues.[266] One of the main recommendations in the field of EAP is that management (at all levels) should positively "support and encourage the programme, supervisors identify and refer troubled employees, trainers need to incorporate EAP training into existing programmes, and employees have to use the programme".[267] There is also a need for active involvement from the highest levels of management or corporate structures in the organisation if EAPs are to succeed. It is standard practice for EAP practitioners to present orientation sessions to supervisors if they wish to engage management. Managers may also attend some of the orientation, information and training sessions scheduled for employees or supervisors. In addition to discussions aimed at familiarising supervisors and managers with the range of services EAPs offer, certain organisations now present targeted training on how to manage employees from different generations, which is proving popular and particularly helpful.

Mogorosi[268] indicated that engagement and capacity building – as regards EAPs – can be incorporated into general supervisor training which should focus on the following:

- An emphasis on management's programme support.
- An explanation of the supervisors' role in programme implementation.
- A demonstration of how programmes can be helpful to supervisors and managers in terms of their job responsibilities.

Another way in which to demonstrate engagement involves visible leadership (i.e., active leadership participation). This implies that management should take the lead in making use of the various programmes and services offered, effectively giving them their personal stamp of approval. Their participation will undoubtedly inculcate a subtle element of trust, which impacts on the crucial issue of confidentiality. This aspect of participation and engagement is particularly relevant to HIV/Aids-related programmes, where employees fear discrimination and being ostracised. Leadership should face up to those fears first, if they expect their employees to follow suit. Organisational leadership is always carefully watched, thus leaders set the tone in terms of the extent to which any policy or programme is supported.[269]

In summary: when management and leadership are engaged in EAPs there is evidence of the following in organisations:

- Improved leadership commitment to such programmes.
- Adequate budgets and resources for these interventions.
- Clear and unambiguous communication from EAP practitioners to personnel.
- Management participation in and dedication to EAPs through carefully constructed performance agreements.
- The development of an overarching policy.

EAP MARKETING PLAN

This section focuses on the purpose or objectives of marketing EAPs. Once the purpose has been established, it is easier to determine possible ways of marketing the programme to ensure that it will be used (effectively) within the organisation.

Objectives of an EAP marketing plan

According to Rajin,[270] marketing plays an important role because it keeps employees and employers informed, creates awareness, and determines the rate at which employees can make use of EAP services. When employees do not know about existing EAPs or how to access them, there is little point in offering such programmes. The objective of a marketing plan is good communication, which should essentially relay an understandable message about EAPs – messages that reach their target audience. Govender[271] noted that the goals of marketing EAPs include informing employees about the purpose of the EAP, identifying the target audience such services are aimed at, providing guidelines on how employees can access these services, and offering explanations to dismiss perceptions that taking part in an EAP invites stigmatisation.

Other objectives in marketing EAPs[272] are to:

- increase employees' knowledge of the EAP and its services;
- increase familiarity and comfort with an EAP's operations and enhance the acceptance and use of the service;
- increase utilisation of the programme services;
- enhance the integration of the EAP within the host or contract organisation and promote a feeling of ownership by all stakeholders (managers, other staff and employees); and
- maintain the visibility of the EAP and its presence as a vital contributor to the organisation's productivity, as well as employees' efficiency, work-life balance and wellbeing.

Marketing EAP services is a basic function of EAP practitioners.[273] The main issues that influence effective communication about the benefits of EAPs in organisations (as identified by employees and practitioners) are clarity, understanding, conciseness, interaction and participation. EAP utilisation is crucial to its success, therefore it is vital to increase the visibility of such programmes and to mainstream EAP services within the core functioning of the organisation – all integral functions of the marketing division.[274] Given the scope of the services on offer, it is expected that a substantive range of people will use individual EAPs. Csiernik and Csiernik[275] indicated that utilisation fluctuates depending on historic issues such as labour-management relations; who began the EAP; the level of orientation, education and promotion surrounding the programme; and any critical incidents that historically (or recently) affected the workforce.

The marketing process

In South Africa, the use of EAPs has grown remarkably within a short space of time;[276] their use has been enhanced through the proper development of training activities (supervisory training and the upskilling of EAP professionals) and improved marketing skills. The marketing of EAPs plays a significant role in their development and acceptance in organisations, therefore the process needs to be effective if the aim is to inform the entire employee cohort about the available services.[277]

Mogorosi[278] noted that the marketing of an EAP should be educational in nature and should utilise various educational fora (e.g. posters and new employee induction/orientation sessions or information/workshop sessions with supervisors, union representatives and/or employee associations). Various techniques used in marketing EAPs include:

- induction and orientation courses;
- posters;
- introductory meetings;
- newsletters;
- the training of supervisors;
- videos;
- meetings with workforce representatives; and
- employer guidelines or codes of conduct.

Managers are responsible for marketing the services that EAPs offer; their benefits can be communicated in the employee handbook or via articles which counsellors publish in the employer's newsletter.[279] There are many different ways of communicating EAP services among employees, including memos, e-mails, brochures, posters, slides and films, which should be accessible to all employees. Mogorosi[280] asserted that information about the available services can also be disseminated by other departments, such as human resources and/or the on-site clinic, which is likely to be in constant contact with employees. Actively promoting the availability of EAPs to employees, their family members and work organisations is the crux of marketing.[281]

Marketing the programme involves promoting it to the leadership, staff and other employees by informing them of existing or new programme services. For the programme to be accessible and effective there is thus a need to "market" it constantly across all levels of the organisation,[282] and the marketing process must include an effective internal communication strategy. Roberts[283] argued that employers can use three ways to promote the use of EAPs amongst employees, namely:

- promoting EAP services at regular intervals through communication (e.g. SMSes and helpline numbers);
- establishing a variety of touch points, i.e., providing EAP services at different times and linking them with employee benefits such as insurance policies; and

- promoting the key message of providing emotional support to employees, which helps remove the stigma surrounding EAPs. The use of case studies in promoting those services that are most appealing to employees can bring such services to life.

Marketing as communication from a management perspective refers to the process of communicating EAP strategies down the respective organisational levels and having them understood and implemented, as well as receiving feedback from employees about their experiences. Nagesar[284] recommended that multiple methods of marketing and communication be used, and that an inclusive approach be followed. A clear line of communication between the upper and lower echelons can prevent numerous implementation and utilisation problems.

For EAPs to attract new/young employees, marketing efforts should use streamlined fonts, bright colours, modern design elements and contemporary messages. EAP practitioners also need to establish methods of calling attention to their services in such a way that clients will make appropriate use of those services; "[A]ny new or unorthodox program must identify avenues to convey its presence, purposes and usefulness" as "no program can survive without visibility, recognition and exposure".[285]

Many EAPs' promotional materials are being redesigned (websites, posters, brochures, wallet cards, other printed material) to be more appealing to younger employees. Websites in particular can be an effective means of communicating about, and promoting, EAPs in an organisation.[286] Where the role of EAPs is communicated as an empowerment function within the organisation, which can improve the functioning of employees, EAPs are able to play a more proactive role in ensuring higher levels of productivity.

CONCLUSION

Knowing the relevant/key stakeholders in an organisation can enable an EAP manager or practitioner to engage with them, so as to gain their support for initiating and implementing related programmes. A marketing plan and strategy are essential for creating awareness and increasing employee uptake of any assistance programmes on offer. In the next chapter, the critical aspects of EAP implementation are concluded with a discussion of the ethical considerations involved.

Chapter 6

ETHICAL CONSIDERATIONS FOR IMPLEMENTING AN EAP

INTRODUCTION

Knowledge about, and the management of, ethical considerations are crucial for the credible implementation of an EAP in any organisation. The scope and context of this chapter focus on how a practitioner or manager can comply with the relevant professional ethics in providing EAP services, where protecting the rights of employees (as users of EAPs) is crucial.

ETHICAL CONSIDERATIONS IN THE IMPLEMENTATION OF EAPs

Ethical codes are based on the premise that professionals have a judiciary or special responsibility towards their clients, due to the unique nature of helping relationships combining both high-minded ethical principles as well as elements of criminal law. Chase[287] indicated that a code of ethics is a contract between professionals that emerges when an occupation becomes recognised in a formal manner, with individuals sharing moral ideals regarding their contribution to the common good. Professionals tend to define ethics by disproportionately emphasising their personal beliefs, virtues and value systems.[288] When they describe the ethical thing to do in their profession, they refer to a personal sense of morality that guides their behaviour in their everyday lives – this makes little reference to the laws, rules or standards governing the profession. Hence, a profession is to be understood as serving to differentiate work that cannot count as such, unless pursued ethically.[289] The following sections describe the ethical codes or principles operating in EAPs.

EAP ethical principles

Govender[290] indicated that ethical standards focus on human behaviours and motivations that work towards the highest ideals of human interaction. Over the past century, various counselling professions have emerged, and with them have come professional codes of ethical conduct.[291] Acting responsibly means showing respect for the ethical obligations and responsibilities which are characteristic of a profession.[292] In this regard, the EAPA, as a professional association, has developed its own ethical principles which agree substantially on which actions constitute ethical and unethical behaviour on the part of practitioners. Hence, all practitioners should accept their profession's ethical codes and should act ethically in seeking approaches which will benefit the unique life situation of each client.[293]

According to the EAP Code of Ethics,[294] ethical principles include the following:

- Service: EAP practitioners routinely provide consultation services to employees, organisations and other stakeholders (such as labour unions), which are aimed at enhancing productivity and safety. Their focus is on minimising work-related and personal problems through their service.
- Beneficence: EAP practitioners protect the welfare and rights of their clients through their diligent work. They avoid or minimise harm and any possible conflicts.
- Fidelity: they establish relationships of trust with those whom they serve, given that individuals who are faced with difficult situations are in need of counselling. The role of the practitioner includes conflict management aimed at preventing harm or exploitation.
- Integrity: it is the responsibility of EAP practitioners to maintain and promote high standards of practice, and to provide clarity in terms of their professional boundaries. These professionals are obligated to advance the values, knowledge and purpose of their profession.
- Respect for clients: practitioners respect their clients and value their right to privacy and confidentiality. They acknowledge and respect individuals' differences with regard to gender, race, colour, ethnicity, culture, national origin, religion, age, sexual orientation and disability.
- Competence: the aim of EAP practitioners is to remain proficient in performing professional activities, and in their practice at large. Since they provide services that reflect their professional competence, these professionals need to keep abreast of the times in terms of EAP trends, the latest research, new technologies and international and local developments.

In addition to the above, **voluntary participation** in EAPs is important. A programme's services need to be provided in a climate which is free from any form of coercion, and where all users are treated equally.[295] This suggests that employees should feel that they are not compelled to consult the programme, and that even though they may make use of such services, they have a right to disengage when they want to.

Organisations thus have to incorporate ethical guidelines in their policies. An example is the core principles of the EAP, as defined within the broader public service that is applicable to the SAPS context. These include:[296]

- ethics and confidentiality (promoting ethical conduct and confidentiality);
- accessibility and a focus on all levels of employment eligibility (full access and capacity at all levels);

- flexibility and adaptability (promoting customised solutions that are department, cluster and sector specific);
- contextual difference (a development thrust that is responsive to organisational circumstances);
- performance focus (training must result in enhanced performance and service delivery); and
- learning communities and organisations (expanding access to knowledge and promoting individual responsibility for learning).

The abovementioned principles are somewhat generic and common within the environment of services provided by employee assistance professionals, such as psychologists, social workers and chaplains (HPCSA, 2012:1). Any related professional who attends to SAPS employees and their immediate families has to abide by a code of ethics.

Responsibilities of EAP practitioners

EAP practitioners have a responsibility to be **ethical to employees as clients,** by abiding by the following guidelines:

- Informed consent: it is the responsibility of EAP professionals to communicate with their clients about how the process will unfold during assessment, referral and follow-up.
- Privacy and confidentiality: EAP professionals are expected to handle clients' information with a high degree of privacy and confidentiality. Information about clients may not be disclosed unless the practitioner is forced by law, written consent was granted by the client, or withholding the information will put the client in danger.
- Screening and assessment: practitioners are only expected to provide services in their areas of specialisation. It is therefore of the utmost importance that they recognise the boundaries of their discipline and area of competence.
- Referrals: the code of professional ethics allows EAP practitioners to refer clients to other professionals with the appropriate expertise, education, credentials and competence to assess and treat the client's problem. Practitioners are not allowed to accept any money, contributions of any nature, or gifts for referrals made.
- Follow-up: EAP professionals must follow up on a client's progress, until all issues of concern have been properly addressed.
- Sexual conduct: it is unethical for EAP professionals to be in sexual relationships with their clients. This includes former clients who received treatment within a period of five years.
- Professional competence: practitioners are expected to practice within their area of expertise and to participate in continued education.

- Representation of qualifications: these professionals are expected to disclose any qualifications or certifications received outside of the EAP profession. When in an EAP role, it is their responsibility to adhere to the EAPA Code of Ethics in dealing with EAP-related matters.
- Non-discrimination: it is unethical for EAP professionals to discriminate against employees in respect of race, colour, ethnicity, religion, national origin, culture, marital status, education, political affiliation, disability, gender or sexual orientation, or age.
- Avoiding harm: EAP professionals are expected to conduct themselves in ways that are not harmful to employees, employers or the communities they serve. It is their responsibility to preserve human life.
- Full disclosure: the onus is on practitioners to fully disclose the purpose and functions of their programme to clients, along with any non-professional or dual relationships, possible conflicts of interest, as well as financial arrangements made with providers and other professionals.
- Delivering EAP services via telephone or other remote technologies: when using emails or SMSes, etc., practitioners should seek adequate training prior to offering their services. Doing so will protect their clients' confidentiality and remove any time barriers.

EAP practitioners are expected to be **ethical as professionals**, therefore they must register and maintain their registration with their respective statutory and/or professional councils, and adhere to the codes of practice of those bodies.[297] Interestingly, codes of ethics reflect the ambivalence of professionalism itself; they hold professionals accountable, while at the same time protecting them from moral accountability.[298] Table 6.1 reflects practitioners' ethical responsibilities towards their profession.

Table 6.1: EAP Code of Ethics (2009)

Responsibility	**Description**
Boundaries of competence	The competence of EAP professionals includes being knowledgeable about their clients, the government laws and regulations, EAP policies and professional standards.
Continuing education and training	It is their responsibility to maintain and enhance their proficiency and competence through participation in continued education and training programs.
Supervision, consultation and advisement	EAP professionals are responsible for providing supervision, and consultation within their scope and range of competence.

Responsibility	Description
Integrity	They maintain integrity by not deceiving others through falsified qualifications and competencies.
Acknowledging credit	When working in collaborations, they have a professional responsibility to recognize and acknowledge the contributions made by others.

Source: EAP (2009:869)

EAP practitioners have a responsibility to be **ethical towards their colleagues and other professionals**. Below is a list of their responsibilities in this regard:

- Interdisciplinary teamwork and collaboration: professionals who serve on interdisciplinary committees or teams are able to maintain the values and standards of their profession. They must pursue appropriate means to resolve any issues of ethical concern.
- Confidential information between colleagues: it is the responsibility of EAP professionals to keep clients' information confidential, unless forced to reveal details by law. Where the practitioner has to consult with colleagues, that should be done in the best interests of the client.
- Respect: it is vital to respect and not denigrate other professionals, or the skills/qualifications of colleagues.
- Disputes: when dealing with disputes, EAP professionals are expected to be fair, accurate and respectful. They should never allow disputes to get in the way of their clients' interests.
- Impairment of colleagues: in a case where a colleague is impaired, EAP professionals are required to assist with appropriate assessment and treatment, and to ensure that such a colleague is prevented from offering EAP services.
- Incompetence of colleagues: practitioners must ensure that incompetent colleagues refrain from offering services to clients in need.
- Responsibility to supervisees and interns: the relationship between EAP professionals and their supervisees/interns should remain professional. Sexual relations with those under supervision are considered unethical.
- Non-discrimination: it is imperative that practitioners comply with all legislation and employment laws. They should offer equal opportunity to all, and not discriminate on the basis of race, gender, colour, ethnicity, religion, national origin, political affiliation, disability, sexual orientation, age, marital status or education.

EAPs are likely to be effective only if employees trust that any services are provided within the appropriate professional boundaries of confidentiality and privacy. When an employee consults an EAP practitioner, a confidential record is opened. Mogorosi[299] added that employees' fear of broken confidences stems from concerns that co-workers will learn about their problems, or that management will use private information to make unfair decisions.

With regard to privacy, in South Africa the Protection of Personal Information Act, 4 of 2013 (POPIA) protects individuals against the unlawful dissemination, collection and storage of personal information without consent. Da Veiga[300] stated that personal information not only relates to an individual's name, surname, age, gender, race, contact information and residential details, but also includes data pertaining to their wellbeing, opinions, views and preferences. This principle requires that EAP practitioners keep a record of each employee in the strictest of confidence, and that they do not disclose such information to any unauthorised person.

It bears reiterating that, without a strongly perceived sense of confidentiality, employees will be hesitant to make use of EAPs. To allow organisations to operate in an ethical manner, appropriate protocols for privacy and confidentiality should be in place.[301] The principle of confidentiality in the application of EAPs is one of the obstacles that make employees hesitant about consulting such programmes, mainly for fear of personal information being leaked.[302]

Confidentiality can be promoted by:

- allowing for guidance in respect of maintaining anonymity, e.g. via telephone calls;
- emphasising the protection of employees' identities and their subsequent rights should any breach occur;
- explaining the practical protection employees will receive, such as locked folder cabinets, using employee numbers as opposed to their names, etc.;
- ensuring that the layout of the EAP office or the interactions of staff do not inadvertently identify an employee or reveal his/her problem; and
- ensuring that issues of confidentiality are dealt with through the use of an off-site wellness centre.

Practitioners must file details about their consultations and the identities of their clients themselves, rather than delegating such duties (e.g. to the human resources management department or registry offices). Practitioners are responsible for establishing the risk of personal information being exposed, and for implementing the necessary controls to mitigate it, for maintaining confidentiality and upholding the right to privacy.[303] Sources of confidentiality protection are found in both legal statutes and codes of professional ethics, which provide guidelines on how and when to disclose confidential information. Rajin[304] stated that many professions view the disclosure of information to unauthorised persons as a serious transgression of the codes of conduct, as well as a punishable act. Employees must thus be guaranteed that confidentiality will be maintained throughout, on every level of the programme.[305]

Confidentiality applies to a professional's obligation to maintain, in confidence, therapeutic or consultative information about clients and their personal problems. There are, however, limits to the confidentiality of records, including the following:

- The requirement, by law and/or professional obligation, for the EAP coordinator to report abuse or negligence on issues such as child abuse.
- The disclosure of records to an external professional adviser for the purpose of ensuring that the required assistance is continued.
- Reporting on situations which are deemed potentially "life threatening" (when there is evidence to raise serious concerns about the physical wellbeing and safety of the employee, or about others who may be threatened by him/her).
- Compliance with a court order or subpoena.

Responsibilities and rights of employees

Employees using EAPs are also expected to conduct themselves appropriately and to know their responsibilities in the process of service delivery.

The following are employees' rights and responsibilities pertaining to EAPs:

- Personal information concerning participation in the EAP is maintained in a confidential manner.
- Participation in the EAP shall not jeopardise an employee's job, nor prejudice any opportunity for promotion or advancement.
- Leave and time off shall be granted in accordance with the organisation's standard policies and procedures for professional assessment, counselling and treatment.
- Employees must take full responsibility for their own health and fully participate in the programme.
- It is the responsibility of the employee to maintain satisfactory job performance.
- Policies define criteria for "additional" treatment emanating from the application of EAPs. These criteria take into consideration whether an employee has a medical aid or not, and the affordability of additional treatment.

In addition to the above, employees have the following rights:

- Personal information concerning participants is to be maintained in a confidential manner. No information related to an employee's participation in the programme is entered in his/her personnel file. Only coded files are used by EAP personnel. An employee may review his/her EAP file at any reasonable time. That file is to be destroyed after seven years of inactivity, or at the request of the employee.
- Participation in the EAP shall not prejudice any opportunity for promotion or advancement.
- The employee shall have the right to paid leave for any EAP assessment. Additional leave may be granted in accordance with the respective collective agreements and/or terms and conditions of employment.
- It is the responsibility of the employee to maintain satisfactory job performance. If personal problems cause his/her work to deteriorate, the employee has a responsibility to obtain the necessary help to bring his/her job performance up to an acceptable level. The EAP provides the means to obtain this help.

Responsibilities of managers and supervisors

As stated earlier, organisations must ensure that participation in an EAP will not jeopardise an employee's job security, compensation or promotional opportunities.[306]

The responsibilities of managers and supervisors include the following:

- Addressing work performance problems through normal supervisory procedures.
- Being consistent and treating employees fairly.
- Ensuring the early identification, management and referral of troubled employees.
- Providing follow-up support to employees when they return to work (if appropriate).
- Not diagnosing the personal problems of the employee.
- Making employees aware of any EAPs that are available in instances where declining job performance has been determined (if appropriate).
- Providing follow-up and support to employees upon their return to work.
- Not requiring the employee to divulge the nature of problems when s/he requests leave for an appointment with the EAP practitioner. If necessary, s/he can provide verification of session attendance through the EAP counsellor.
- Maintaining a strict level of confidentiality in all cases.

Union responsibilities

Unions, as key stakeholders in the implementation of EAPs, also have responsibilities. It is incumbent upon unions to ensure ethical service delivery by:

- being knowledgeable about the programmes and referral procedures;
- encouraging members to use the EAPs; and
- maintaining a strict level of confidentiality in all cases.

ETHICAL DILEMMAS

It is important to understand the nature of the ethical dilemmas an EAP practitioner might encounter. Competency to practice and help clients with many different issues can raise unexpected ethical dilemmas. Thus, difficult issues (such as the need to protect anyone whom a client threatens to harm) require focused attention and usually have complex solutions.[307] Practitioners in this profession frequently encounter ethical dilemmas, hence the percentage of ethics complaints and violations has remained constant over the past decades. Chase[308] questioned why a profession, which is so immersed in intellectual accountability and ethical decision-making, continues to experience ethical violations in many of the same areas of practice. While the solution remains debatable, being able to deal with dilemmas can prevent the practitioner from behaving unethically in the process of delivering a service.

Nature of ethical dilemmas

The implementation of an assistance programme is not immune to ethical dilemmas. EAP practitioners face increasingly complex scenarios, as communities and societies battle to cope with increasingly scarce resources and greater demands being placed on employees across all sectors. Numerous different and complex ethical dilemmas may arise to confront practitioners at times when an ethical code is insufficient or offers them little direction on how to proceed. Practitioners have:

- the duty to warn clients;
- to promote voluntary participation; and
- to encourage informed consent.

At times, ethical codes may conflict with the law and cause a dilemma for the practitioner. For example, on a basic level, the codes may require confidentiality, while the law on child abuse requires that confidentiality be broken, even where there is no imminent danger.[309] Govender[310] argued that some of the ethical issues or dilemmas relating to EAP practice deal with:

- privacy and confidentiality;
- a conflict of interest (balancing the interests of the individual client against those of the organisation);
- informed consent;
- the termination of service (does it end when the employee no longer works for the employer?);
- the competence of EAP practitioners/contractors/referral resources;
- the shift to cost containment/managed care;
- the loss of boundaries around employee assistance functions and competencies; and
- a misrepresentation in marketing/advertising.

Articulating the relationship between moral reasoning and the influence of environmental factors (e.g. organisational culture, resource allocation and availability) may add a useful dimension to addressing ethical dilemmas.[311] The next section focuses on managing ethical dilemmas in practice.

Dealing with ethical dilemmas

Ethical dilemmas are complex in nature, however ethical codes and country laws provide an initial direction for an EAP practitioner against which to evaluate his/her moral intuition. Professional organisations establish ethical codes to guide practitioners' behaviour and decision-making.[312] The EAPA Code of Ethics is one level of justification in the decision-making process which practitioners can refer to when confronted with ethical dilemmas while delivering EAP services. To be effective, a decision-making model should preserve employee privacy and confidentiality.[313] Yet, following rules without considering the possibility of exceptions or the context of broader principles can create barriers between clients and practitioners, and may cause the latter to miss opportunities to improve their relationships with the former and facilitate positive outcomes.[314]

Peer influence is arguably a stronger determinant of ethical behaviour than practitioners' affective reactions.[315] This implies that the work environment plays a critical role in ethical decision-making. An environment can be a significant factor in helping practitioners to develop moral sensitivity and a moral character. According to Chase,[316] ethical decision-making includes moral sensitivity (recognising a moral dilemma), moral judgement (deciding whether an action is right or wrong), moral motivation (prioritising moral values over other values, so as to develop moral intention) and moral character (having the courage to act in a manner that is consistent with moral intentions). The question is: What are professional ethics concerned with, if not with morality? This implies that morality is central to dealing with ethical dilemmas.

Schwandt[317] suggested that this involves cultivating capacities in moral reasoning, including a moral imagination and moral sensitivity (i.e., recognising the moral issue at stake), as well as an ability to recognise flawed moral arguments. Both ethics and morality are used in professional integrity. In the moral sense, ethics refers to the social system of ethics application, but morals determine individual character. This implies that morality, unlike ethics, overrides all other considerations – it cannot be measured against any other criterion, not least because there is nothing other than itself by which morality can be measured.[318]

According to Mines et al.,[319] there are "tiers of justification" in ethical decision-making when dealing with a specific related dilemma:

- The first tier is that of moral intuition, which includes the gathering of facts and development of moral sensitivity. At times, this level of reasoning may be sufficient and/or necessary. In instances of immediate action, the EAP provider does not have the luxury of time and reflection. Petitions by a client may sway the EAP provider away from his moral sense of what is ethical. When situations like this occur, it is necessary for the EAP provider to enter into more of a reflective thinking process.
- The second tier is the critical evaluative level of reasoning. At this level, the EAP provider can "evaluate or justify his ordinary moral judgements". This level is hierarchical and includes (1) rules, professional codes, or law; and (2) ethical principles.

The first/intuitive level is used when quick action is necessary, and includes practical decision-making that involves deciding what ought to be done now, in this situation, given this set of circumstances.[320] Knapp, Handelsman, Gottlieb and Vandecreek[321] indicated that "ethical" contains a number of modifiers, such as "reasonable," "appropriate", "to the extent possible" and so forth, in recognition of the need for professional judgement in unique circumstances or unusual situations. This level of decision-making suggests that discretion needs to be used in dealing with ethical dilemmas. This judgement or discernment "involves understanding both *that* and *how* principles and rules apply in a variety of dilemma situations".[322]

At the second level, the EAP practitioner can consult professional ethical codes to gauge his/her moral intuition. Where the codes are not adequate or are in conflict, the next level of ethical principles can be utilised, as the practitioner works through unstructured ethical dilemmas. Brecher[323] noted that a code is a set of rules; some may take the form of advice rather than direction, but despite this, they remain rules. It is important to apply the code of ethics in decision-making. Decisions about what is correct and right to do have a normative foundation, i.e., they involve value judgements.[324] Codes as rules are formulae, and following the rules as a means of making the right decision is a matter of looking up the appropriate rule in the relevant handbook.[325] This means that it involves acting rationally in situations demanding practical decisions, where action means attending to both empirical and normative considerations.

Ethical violations

Failure to deal with an ethical dilemma normally leads to ethical violations and complaints. Some practitioner psychologists clearly act inappropriately, whether out of misguided benevolence, selfishness, impulsivity or some other motive. Most ethical violations occur because practitioners simply do not know the laws or standards governing their profession.[326] Major types of dilemmas and complaints fall under the umbrella of questionable ethics, included the firing of employees, personnel practice violations and breaches of contracts.[327] Brecher[328] argued that professional ethics offers a way of avoiding these issues, rather than facing them. When a dilemma presents itself, the first rule of professional ethics in practice is to reduce tensions and then to successfully assist in achieving an effective response.

As a practitioner, it is crucial to respond to a dilemma with prudence, modesty and receptivity to feedback – this demands an acknowledgement that all of us have blind spots that can lead us to act in a less than optimal manner, for reasons outside of our conscious awareness.[329] Professional ethics and practice, in fact, are structural systems that are integrated to assist practitioners to recognise the potential dilemma and to discover accurate solutions to deal with dilemmas.[330] Practitioners thus need to be cognisant of the fact that everyone makes mistakes, and when they do, they should acknowledge this and try to correct them. Certain instances of ethical decision-making – especially when practitioners are distressed – will fall outside of their conscious awareness, but if they are alert to this fact, they may still be able to act ethically.

The best way to prevent ethical violations is by creating an ethical organisational culture. When an organisation rewards ethical behaviour through its organisational culture, the reward has a great influence on a practitioner's ethical decision-making.[331] Culture encourages accountability as a "condition of accountability", in particular, an obligation or a willingness to accept individual responsibility for personal actions.[332] An ethical culture in EAP practice is based on developed standards because they promote the wellbeing of clients, respect their autonomy, and work towards fair treatment and/or other overarching ethical goals. Knapp et al.[333] argued that even though each employee has at some stage encountered a colleague who acted in a questionable way, they perceive themselves as behaving ethically, or at times even consider their own behaviour to be exemplary. Organisational culture should thus be used constructively to prevent and discourage ethical violations in EAP practice.

A record of ethical dilemmas and complaints is needed for the further training of practitioners and for the purposes of prevention. Training and raising awareness on ethical violations are important, because all people are vulnerable to "ordinary ethical lapses" in which they perform in a less-than-optimal manner, often without being aware of their own shortcomings. Sfestani and Peykani[334] explained that a professional is actually a structural and functional system who tries to identify potential conflicts and offer suitable solutions.

The recommendation is that a database be developed to enable the systemic study of ethical infractions, and to standardise reports so that data can be collected in uniform categories.[335] Moral decision-making and moral action have to be internalised.[336] The complexity of professional practice requires discretion in terms of how to interpret and implement many of the ethical codes currently in use. As part of their lifelong education in ethics, practitioners and managers need to pursue humility, use think-aloud processes, and welcome feedback to improve their own ethical conduct, as well as ethical conduct in their practices.

CONCLUSION

This chapter on ethical considerations concludes the process of EAP initiation and implementation in organisations. Any practitioner or manager should be guided by ethical codes or principles in their daily practice, as that will guarantee that EAP services are offered and delivered with integrity. The ability to identify ethical dilemmas and deal with them is crucial for the success of any EAP practice.

Chapter 7

DEVELOPMENT OF AN EAP POLICY AND PROCEDURES

THE NEED FOR AN EAP POLICY

The existence of an EAP policy is important in organisations because of the developments in this field. Historically, EAPs began in the 1940s, with a focus on the effect of the use and abuse of alcohol on job performance. Over time, the emphasis broadened to include other personal issues that may have an impact on job performance. EAP services grew tremendously in the early 1970s to help employees address a variety of problems and to proactively deal with workplace issues that may lead to workplace violence, physical and mental health issues, or declining morale among employees.

According to Lewis and Lewis,[337] the central purpose of an EAP is to provide timely, professional aid to people whose personal problems at work, at home and in the community at large might otherwise lead to a deterioration in work performance, absenteeism, accidents, conflicts in the work setting, or even job termination.

Over the past decade, the field of employee assistance has grown significantly in addressing complex employee and behavioural health issues, including work-life balance challenges. Today most EAPs are designed to support multiple kinds of employee, family and workforce performance issues. EAPs have expanded to deal with not only mental health and substance issues, but also with health and wellness and work-life types of concerns. One facet of EAPs is their focus on the individual employee and their family members, while another facet is the role of the organisation, which may include prevention, training, consultation, organisational development and crisis response services. Some companies follow a comprehensive approach to corporate wellness and develop a culture that encourages a healthy lifestyle.[338]

A policy is an instrument that demonstrates the organisation's support and endorsement. If it is well constructed, it enables successful programme administration, but if poorly conceived and established, it can cause the EAP to fail. Govender[339] asserted that while the policy is important, it is not sufficient to guarantee success. A policy must be put into operation to be effective, and its services must be compatible with performance appraisal systems, grievance processes, disciplinary procedures, insurance policies and, above all, the protection of employee privacy through strict confidentiality, in order for the EAP to be viable.

A model of an EAP policy

A model of an EAP policy should include a statement to assist the organisation and cover the following: an explanatory introduction; the company's view on personal problems and the role of the EAP within the organisation; the goals of the EAP; the responsibilities of the EAP; the role of management, the unions and employees; policy disclaimers; EAP procedures; the location of the EAP; EAP staff; and EAP records and evaluations.

Research conducted in some government institutions has indicated that an integrated (standardised) employee assistance policy and work practice should be developed to be used as frameworks to address issues such as confidentiality, work processes and procedures, and ethical conduct for psychologists, social workers and chaplains.[340] An EAP policy describes the strategic and operational framework for the programme and the implementation thereof; it is the product of a collective effort of all the key stakeholders in the organisation who are committed to and concerned with the effective implementation of the EAP.[341]

Objectives and purpose of the EAP policy

An EAP policy should include the vision, mission and objectives of the programme as part of its strategic focus. To ensure a proper understanding of what the programme is for and how it operates, the vision, mission and objectives should be prominently displayed and distributed within the targeted population of an organisation.[342]

The following aspects of the policy covering the purpose and objectives can be communicated using wall poster statements and pamphlets, and can be incorporated into staff orientations, inductions and general information booklets:

Vision

The term "vision" is often also broadly referred to as personal agenda, purpose, legacy, dream or goal. The vision indicates the core values and can distinguish organisations from each other. Ford and Pasmore[343] defined vision as a statement of purpose which is determined by management and based on the organisation's core values and beliefs that define the organisation's identity.

An EAP that is aligned with the organisational values and vision will measurably enhance and promote business operations, the overall employee experience, and the perceptions of the community of the organisation. A well-run EAP, to realise its vision, will produce a positive return on investment.[344]

Mission

EAPs provide strategic analyses, recommendations, and consultations throughout an organisation to enhance its performance, culture, and business success. These enhancements are accomplished by professionally trained behavioural and/or psychological experts who apply the principles of human behaviour to management, employees and their families, as well as workplace situations, to optimise the organisation's human capital.[345]

The mission statement is usually depicted as the starting point in the strategic planning process; the content of the mission statement should correspond to its intended functions. The primary components of the mission are the purpose, principle business aims, corporate identity, policies and values of the organisation.

The basic function of the mission statement is to provide a more focused basis for resource allocation, motivating members within the organisation to achieve a common goal or purpose, creating performance standards, providing a common purpose or direction, and developing shared values within the organisation.

The mission of the EAP is to contribute toward the total health of employees in order to have a productive and satisfied workforce. This is accomplished in a twofold manner:

1. Through confidential counselling offered to employees whose job performance is (or has the potential to be) adversely affected by personal or work-related stress.
2. Through timely group sessions focusing on wellness programming delivered at the work site.

Objectives

The objectives the organisation intends to achieve with the introduction of an EAP policy should be articulated. The most common objectives incorporated in EAP policies are:

1. To provide constructive assistance to employees and their immediate family members who are experiencing any form of personal problems such as physical illness, mental and emotional illness, family distress, financial problems, alcoholism, drug dependency, legal issues or others.
2. To render a confidential service aimed at assisting employees by helping them to improve their efficiency and quality of life by means of preventative and remedial activities.
3. To timeously identify, assess and refer troubled employees/underachievers for specialist treatment (by internal or external service providers) for successful re-integration into the work environment.

4. To prevent a decline in performance from employees with normally satisfying job performance and potential.
5. To establish and maintain a holistic approach to remedy personal, social and emotional problems.
6. To increase the level of interpersonal skills exhibited amongst employees in the organisation.
7. To enhance the quality of life of all employees.
8. To provide employees with a fulfilling, safe and healthy working environment.

A practical example

Research conducted by Grobler and Joubert[346] in the public service, and specifically the South African Police Service (SAPS), highlighted some of the important principles of EAPs. The authors[347] defined the core of the EAP in the SAPS within the broader public service as follows:

- Ethics and confidentiality (promoting ethical conduct and confidentiality).
- Accessibility and focus on all levels of employment eligibility (full access and capacity at all levels).
- Flexibility and adaptability (promoting customised solutions that are department-, cluster- and sector-specific).
- Contextual difference (developing trust that is responsive to organisational circumstances).
- Performance focus (training must result in enhanced performance and service delivery).
- Learning communities and organisations (expanding access to knowledge and promoting individual responsibility for learning).

The above-mentioned principles are somewhat generic and well-known in the environment of EAP professionals (e.g. psychologists, social workers and chaplains).[348]

The EAP professional who attends to SAPS employees and their immediate families has to abide by a code of ethics. The following are cross-cutting principles in the SAPS EAP (across all professions and registration categories):[349]

- Information regarding services must be available to all employees – they have the right to be informed.
- The EAP must render services to support all employees with a clear understanding of their situation, which in most instances is context-specific.
- Services need to be accessible to all employees, regardless of their rank or status.
- The EAP must be available to employees at all times.

- The EAP must respond immediately when services are requested.
- Confidentiality regarding sensitive and personal information must be maintained at all costs.
- The EAP must behave credibly, in other words, they should lead by example and practice what they preach.
- The EAP must not only focus on the employees' problems (traditional EAP approach), but also focus on empowering them with the necessary skills and knowledge to cope with their day-to-day demands. In other words, the EAP must have a proactive/empowering approach.

In addition to the above, EAPs provide value in the following ways, and therefore the objectives may include:[350]

- Encouraging employee engagement and improving the abilities of employees and their next of kin to successfully respond to life's challenges;
- Offering employees short-term services for problem resolution or referring employees and their next of kin to physical and mental health treatment services when required;
- Developing competencies within the organisation to deal with complex emotional, cultural and diversity issues;
- Decreasing workplace accidents and incidents and assisting in emergency response;
- Reducing workplace absenteeism and unplanned absences and reducing healthcare costs;
- Improving employee morale and thereby lowering employee turnover and costs related to replacement;
- Facilitating effective, safe and timely returns to work for employees after short-term or extended absences;
- Improving the value of organisational investments in health and wellness promotion, self-care management, continuity of healthcare and work-related efforts;
- Increasing the efficient use of healthcare through the process of early identification, care management and recovery efforts;
- Reducing the likelihood of workplace violence and other safety risks;
- Managing the effects of incidents such as workplace violence, injury or other crises, and facilitating a quick return to work after such events;
- Supporting disaster and emergency preparedness in order to minimise disruption after such events;
- Ensuring a smooth transition and adjustment to mergers, acquisitions, site closures and other workforce change events; and

- Reducing the likelihood of legal action or liability to the organisation by maintaining good business practices that promote a healthy and safe workplace.

A practical example is the SAP's EAS (Employee Assistance Support), which was researched by Grobler and Joubert.[351]

GUIDELINES FOR EMPLOYEE PARTICIPATION IN EAPs

A policy document on the EAP should clearly state the guidelines for employee participation; employees and their next of kin should know what is expected of them when using the programme, and what they can expect from service providers/practitioners. The responsibilities of different role players in the application of the EAP must be clearly spelt out.

Employees' responsibilities as recipients of services

The employment contract stipulates that the employer is obligated to pay to the employee a fixed wage and other fringe benefits agreed upon. The benefits include the employer taking financial responsibility for the EAP services provided to employees. More than 75% of American employers provide confidential EAP, short-term counselling services to their workforce, which are paid for by the employer.[352] In return, the employee offers his/her capacity to work. The employer has to convert this capacity into productive activity and is dependent on the employee's availability and skill.

It is in the best interests of both the employer and the employee to actively engage in creating an effective workplace, which will provide support to employees, enabling them to work more efficiently and to achieve a better work-life balance.[353]

Employees' rights and responsibilities in EAPs, which can be included in a policy statement, are discussed in previous chapters.

Benefits that employees and next-of-kin derive from participation

The EAP and work-life fields often share common goals of supporting employees and working families, while also supporting the needs of the employer and the broader workplace. Both of these fields value the importance of work, as well as the notion that one's work life and personal life influence each other. The EAP typically reports to HR or another department within the work organisation, with services being managed internally. However, most of their client-contact services are provided by a network of other contractors, the staff of vendors, or other business partners.

Kanter[354] suggested that work and life cannot be viewed as separate spheres, and EAPs recognise that employees' problems cannot be addressed in a vacuum. As EAPs worked more and more with employee problems, they found that in order to truly support sustained recovery, services had to be expanded to address a variety of work-life concerns that affect individual employees and their families. Therefore, the EAP professional finds herself/himself needing to resolve issues related to childcare, workplace leave policies, and other family concerns.

Many organisations have integrated their EAPs and work-life programmes within the same unit. EAPs and work-life programmes rely on similar methods for service delivery, which includes telephonic assessment and referral, brief intervention, problem resolution and follow-up. These programmes also offer outreaches; education and training programmes; information provided through newsletters, summary sheets and web pages; consultation with managers and supervisors; and programme evaluation.[355]

The benefits employees and their next of kin gain from participating in the EAP are as follows:[356]

1. Improved job performance.
2. Reduced absenteeism.
3. Assistance to resolve personal problems.
4. Increased safety awareness.
5. Reduction in stress-related accidents and incidents.
6. Reduced healthcare costs.
7. Increased productivity.
8. Improved quality of life and the achievement of a work-life balance.
9. Increase in employee morale.

Many organisations also include activities such as workshops, seminars and medical procedures in their wellness programmes. DuBrin[357] listed the following typical components of wellness programmes:

1. Medical examinations comprising a lifestyle questionnaire, blood analysis, flexibility testing, hearing and vision exams, skin inspection, body-fat measurement, blood-pressure screening, and mammograms (screening for breast cancer).
2. Stress management.
3. Weight control (for both overweight and underweight).
4. Smoking cessation programmes.
5. Alcohol and illegal drug control.
6. Substance abuse counselling and referral.

7. Preventive healthcare.
8. Safety on the job and at home.
9. Hypertension (high blood pressure) control.
10. Healthy lifestyle and self-care.

The theory behind work-life balance and the role of EAPs

The theoretical foundation used by industrial and organisational psychologists to study work and family relationships is derived from role theory, which focuses on how individuals in social contexts practice what is expected of their roles or positions. The idea of work-family conflict is derived from the belief that when individuals have to act out multiple roles, psychological distress grows due to the increased conflict that can occur when the expectations of one role, such as work, interfere with the expectations of the other (family) role. Balancing the demands of work and personal life is a major challenge facing the workforce today;[358] many people leave the corporate environment to find such a balance.

Organisational support of work and family roles refers to the degree to which the workplace is designed to reduce work-family conflicts, and to enhance work-family interactions. Work-family policies are organisational programmes, policies and practices which are designed to assist employees to jointly manage a paid work role and non-work roles such as parenting, elder care, leisure, education and self-care (exercise or medical needs). Examples of provisions made by work-family policies include flexibility in work scheduling (flexi-time), location (telework, mobile virtual office), or the amount of work allocated (job sharing, part time work, vacation and leave); benefits such as health, child, domestic partner and elder care; and information, such as referral programmes.

Role expansion theories focus on the positive resource transfer between various roles of an individual (i.e employee, parent, colleague or community member roles) and make the assumption that greater involvement in meaningful roles with positive experiences can promote wellbeing and positive functioning.

Positive organisational psychology also plays a role in employee wellbeing. Donaldson and Ko[359] defined positive organisational psychology as the study of positive subjective experiences and traits in the workplace and positive organisations, and their application to improve the effectiveness and quality of life in other organisations.

A function of EAPs is to focus on work-family role conflict, which is due to the following reasons:

1. More and more families, as well as single working individuals, have to juggle work and caregiving roles.

2. The recent global economic slowdown and the aging population worldwide has resulted in a growing proportion of the population being involved in employment for longer periods of their life span, and having to care for their own health needs.
3. High unemployment rates have highlighted the need for a change in mind-sets to the positive benefits of having a job and an income for an individual's identity, family household economic security, and the greater community.

The process of participation in an EAP

The decision to participate in an EAP must always be **voluntary**. Mogorosi[360] argued that the services of the programme need to be provided in a climate free of any form of coercion, and where all service users are treated equally. This implies that employees and their next of kin should be informed about the programme, yet not feel that they are compelled to make use of it. Further, even though they may be using the services, they have the right to disengage when they want to.

Participation in EAPs can be either self-initiated or employer-initiated. When an offer to participate in an EAP is made, it is neither compulsory nor mandatory for the employee to accept the offer.

1. **Self-initiated participation:** this occurs when an employee recognises that a problem exists and seeks assistance by calling the EAP office directly. This may have resulted from a co-worker, family member, friend, or supervisor being concerned about the employee and informally suggesting the use of the employee assistance programme.
2. **Employer-initiated participation:** an employee is responsible for keeping his/her job performance at an acceptable level. If his/her job performance shows continuing deterioration and informal offers of assistance have not been accepted, then the supervisor may initiate a formal offer of assistance.[361] Prior to initiating a formal offer of assistance, the supervisor should consult with the EAP practitioner about the appropriateness of an offer to participate. A good EAP, established with union buy-in, reinforces the supervisor's responsibilities and creates forums for employee debates.[362] The following steps must govern an employer-initiated offer of assistance:
    - **Informal** – The supervisor must ensure that the employee receives an informal offer of assistance before initiating a formal offer of assistance. Such offers must be documented. (Certain behaviour could result in an employer-initiated offer(s) without there being previous informal offers.)
    - **Formal** – The formal employer-initiated offer of assistance must be in writing on the prescribed form and must include an appointment time with the EAP counsellor. A formal offer of assistance is to be hand-delivered to the employee, with a copy going to

the EAP practitioner and a copy being retained in a confidential "Formal offer of EAP assistance" file.

Some guidelines for employees

Employees can themselves also take several steps to better balance the demands of their work and personal lives. One of the major decisions they can take is to make use of the available EAP programmes. An overview can be found below of the balancing act and some steps that employees can take:

- Plan ahead for family events.
- Discuss work commitments with your partner or prospective partner.
- Become a downshifter (living a simpler life).
- Maintain a buffer between work and home.
- Become a telecommuter.
- Make use of organisational support systems such as an EAP.

Figure 7.1: Adapting work and personal life demands
Source: Adapted from DuBrin[363]

The steps above can be executed in the following ways:

Planning ahead for family events

One of the ways to minimise the conflict between work and family events would be to plan not only your work activities, but also your family activities.

Discussing work commitments with your partner or prospective partner

Conflict about family and work demands can often be prevented if each partner discusses their work schedule with the other. If both agree, or a compromise can be reached, future conflict can be avoided.

Becoming a downshifter

Another possibility is for the employee to negotiate with the employer to choose a different, less demanding career. Many mothers opt for this, as they usually do not want to resign and plan to stay in the organisation until such time as they can again focus on their career.

Maintaining a buffer time between work and home

Commuting between home and work can be very time consuming, especially if one lives in a major city, however this time can be used very effectively to prepare mentally for work or home.

Becoming a telecommuter

Many organisations offer their employees the opportunity to work from home. These programmes are very popular, as they offer employees the opportunity to balance their work and personal lives much better. Some universities offer this opportunity to their senior professors, and research indicates that they are much more productive than their colleagues who work office hours at the university.

Making use of organisational support systems such as EAPs

Many organisations provide EAP programmes or services to their employees, some of which were discussed earlier in the chapter. It is important that employees should identify which of these programmes could be beneficial to them and enrol in those. Figure 7.2 indicates how policies and leadership can create a positive perception of an organisation's support of its EAP.

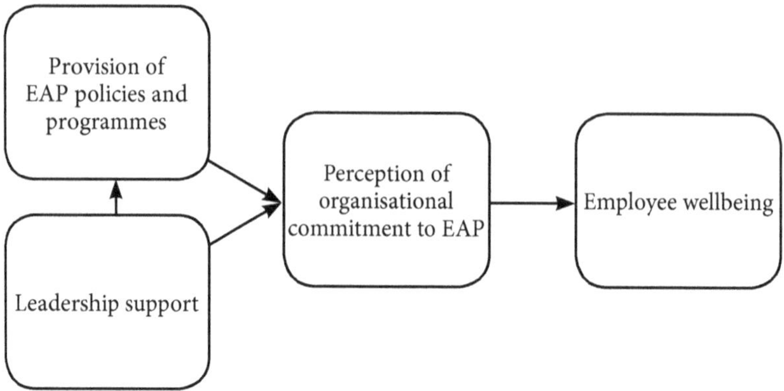

Figure 7.2: Model linking leadership support, the provision of EAP facilities and employee wellbeing
Source: Adapted from Milner, Greylin, Goetzel, Da Silva, Kolber-Alexander, Patel, Nosel and Beckowiski[364]

Organisational support is visible when there are policies and leadership support; the leadership has a role to play in creating an organisational culture of health and wellbeing. Milner et al.[365] argued that perceptions of organisational commitment to health promotion mediate the relationship between the provision of such policies and programmes and employee wellbeing. For this reason it is important for leaders to demonstrate their commitment to employee health by ensuring that their policies and procedures are implemented in the organisation.

CONCLUSION

Central to the use of an EAP and the participation of employees in such a programme is that the policy must highlight that this process is voluntary. Employees and their next of kin should be guided by the policy to make an informed decision about using or participating in EAPs. Apart from the components that should be covered in an EAP policy, this section described the procedure that has to be followed and the types of services offered by an EAP programme. Lastly, the role of employees in balancing work and personal life demands was discussed.

Chapter 8

THE EAP PROCESS/PROCEDURE

An EAP policy should communicate to employees that there is a process that has to be followed in EAP service delivery. This procedure entails the intake, assessment, intervention, evaluation and termination phases. Employees should not expect their EAP services to be a quick fix for their situations/dysfunctions, i.e., they should be informed in the policy that they will have to go through various phases.

The intake or initial phase

The intake phase is also known as the initial referral phase. It is at this stage that employees can consult with EAP practitioners concerning access to the programme, how to raise a concern regarding a co-worker or supervisor experiencing problems, or to ask general questions (e.g. about resources available in the community). During this initial interview, the practitioner will explain the EAP process, including the confidentiality of the programme and the employee's rights and responsibilities.

This phase involves several functions within the organisation – functions which form a network:

1. ***The employee:*** the EAP is designed for the employee and it is of the utmost importance that the employee is aware of his/her responsibility regarding the programme. The employee acts as a self-referral agent; as mentioned earlier, it is important that employees themselves see the value of being involved in an EAP.
2. ***Fellow employees:*** they may have knowledge of a colleague's problem and have the ability to motivate the troubled employee to make use of the EAP. They are secondary referral agents.
3. ***Supervisor:*** the primary function of supervisors is to ensure that their employees are productive. Employees who do not perform according to their potential and expected performance outcomes should be assisted to overcome disabling problems. The EAP intake is dependent on the training, insight and referral of supervisors, to assist and enable employees to function productively.
4. ***Personnel officers and managers:*** one of the functions of personnel officers and managers is to monitor indicators and trends such as the amount of sick leave taken, absenteeism rates, and disciplinary action patterns. These trends should trigger alerts and cases should be referred to the EAP in order to assist an employee to adjust his/her behaviour.

A successful EAP function is one where the troubled employee is identified, motivated and referred to counselling before their impairment affects productivity. Identification, motivation and referral can take place informally or formally, or the individual employee may "refer" himself/herself. The aim is to empower an employee to refer himself/herself for counselling through the EAP system. The procedure of self-referral would involve the employee acknowledging or identifying that they have a problem. The employee needs to be motivated to make an appointment, either in or outside working hours. Informal referrals are done by concerned EAP functions or fellow employees. The procedure is similar to that of self-referral. A formal referral has a different procedure, and the focus is then on unsatisfactory work performance and not necessarily on personal problems.

Management may use a formal referral as a means to provide an employee with a chance to improve work performance, prior to taking disciplinary action. The supervisor needs to motivate the employee, through a formal discussion, to make one of three choices: joint problem-solving by the employee and management; referral to the EAP; or corrective disciplinary action. Should the employee choose the joint problem-solving or the corrective disciplinary option, action would be taken according to the organisation's policy. In the formal referral process, the EAP centre would provide feedback to the manager regarding the following aspects: whether the individual could be assisted by EAP intervention; what the plan of action is; and the progress made in the course of counselling. Confidential and personal information about the employee cannot be shared with the manager without prior written consent from the employee.[366]

The assessment or diagnostic phase

The policy document should describe the assessment or diagnostic phase. The purpose of this phase is to assess the impact that the individual employee's personal, social and economic environment has on her/his functioning, productivity and personal growth.

Some EAPs act as an assessment, short-term service and referral system (if referral is necessary). Assessment provides early recognition of a problem, with the goal being to enable the employee to receive help before a crisis develops. It should be clear from the policy that the EAP is not a method of avoiding discipline, nor is it to be used by management as a disciplinary measure. The intent is, after assessment, to give employees the opportunity to voluntarily seek help with personal problems that may affect their work performance. (See the discussion earlier on the workshops, seminars, activities and medical procedures that can be offered as part of an EAP.)

Assessment should be conducted for employees who have requested assistance under their EAP, so that they can be provided with full information on participation in the programme. During the assessment, the practitioner and employee will take a detailed look at the nature and severity of the problem. Upon completion of the assessment, the practitioner and the employee will discuss the options which appear to be most realistic for the employee in resolving the problem. The employee will choose the treatment service and, if necessary, a referral will be arranged.

The intervention or treatment phase

The intervention/treatment is based on the diagnosis made during the employee assessment. This phase involves the use of EAP strategies and techniques such as counselling, therapy, group work, life-skills development and crisis management. Intervention occurs when practitioners are able to assist employees and their dependants when work performance is threatened. The focus of providing an intervention is re-integrating the troubled employee into his/her work environment as quickly as possible.

Various inputs and resources are required by EAP practitioners for the intervention stage. The following is an indication of what might be needed.

1. ***Material input:*** training material and posters, pamphlets and flyers used as marketing material are necessary to motivate employees to use the service.
2. ***Energy input:*** to implement an EAP, professional expertise and knowledge of human behaviour are required. An EAP is also dependent on the inputs of various people/functions in the organisation, such as the EAP coordinator, the EAP action committee and the supervisors.
3. ***Information input:*** a constant flow of information about the employee or the status of the employee occurs during the process. Information is communicated to the therapist and back to the organisation for the employee to be re-integrated into the system.
4. ***Management input:*** an EAP needs to be managed well to ensure compliance with its principles. This requires planning, organising, leading and control functions, which should be provided by the Board of Directors and the Executive Committee.
5. ***Technology input:*** to facilitate feedback and evaluation, data on the employees taking part in the EAP are captured on a statistical programme. Other technology inputs include professional psychometric assessments, professional software, and expertise in the diagnosis and development of a treatment plan and evaluation outcomes.
6. ***Facilities input:*** counselling centres, on-site clinics, vehicles, computer networks and 24-hour emergency telephone numbers are the facilities required by most EAPs.
7. ***Labour input:*** administrative personnel, an EAP coordinator, an EAP action committee, professional counsellors/therapists and designated trained employees are the labour inputs required for the EAP.

The evaluation or prognosis phase

The policy should point out that employees and practitioners will take part in the process of evaluating the EAP service, thus it is important for practitioners to introduce appropriate measures for monitoring and evaluating the effect of their services at this stage. Such measures will also assist EAP practitioners in monitoring the efficacy of all the programmes they conduct.

Follow-up sessions may be used by practitioners to evaluate the process. This means that EAP practitioners will have to follow up on counselling and awareness programmes to ensure that the information provided during such programmes, and insights arrived at, have long-term effects on people's lives. EAP practitioners can also develop a basic evaluation system that will enable them to effectively report on the status of their services in the organisation. In other words, the practitioner will have to maintain an informal, but planned, follow-up procedure.

Some interesting studies have been conducted to determine to what extent employees use EAP programmes. In a study in the SAPS, some important aspects of the EAP programme were highlighted which may also help other practitioners to focus their programmes:[367]

- The programme (EAP) was well represented in their immediate working environment.
- The participants had very high expectations of the EAP.
- Their experience of the EAP was lower than their perceptions, but higher than their expectations. The EAP personnel were seen as accessible, credible and rendering confidential services.
- The satisfaction levels of some provinces with the EAP were quite low.
- There were differences between the satisfaction levels of different races and rank groups, with the lower ranks being the most dissatisfied.

Some of the important recommendations in this study[368] were that:

- an integrated approach should be used for the implementation of an EAP in order to equip all EAP functionaries with the necessary skills and knowledge to render an integrated service;
- customised orientation and in-house training should be provided to EAP functionaries;
- an integrated EAP policy and work protocol should be developed; and
- special attention needs to be given to the lower ranks.

It is important to note that many of these recommendations align with the guidelines given earlier in this chapter.

In her study, Padachy[369] highlighted some interesting recommendations in a banking environment:

- Any EAP must have an evaluation system which will not only help to continuously improve the programme, but also ensure user satisfaction.
- Post-treatment follow-up is very important.
- An inefficient management information system for the database may lead to lack of confidentiality and it can be a major drawback in the delivery of an EAP.
- Union involvement is very important in an EAP.

In a study by Brink,[370] which determined the extent to which EAPs can be utilised by welfare agencies to ensure that work-related and personal problems do not negatively influence the productivity of social workers, the author found that social workers have a need for services that will prevent, relieve or eliminate their work-related and personal problems in order to improve their productivity and general functioning.

She furthermore found that:

- an EAP should be managed from a humanistic, organisational, cost-effective, effective and labour relations rationale;
- management needs to take responsibility for their EAP; and
- a needs assessment must be conducted to determine what influences employee productivity.

The termination or referral phase

The termination phase should outline how the practitioners will end their services with the employees, as this stage can evoke negative reactions or emotions on the part of employees. It is critical that the practitioner should have the skills and competencies to deal with these emotions.

If an employee has been absent from work due to treatment, then the EAP practitioner should be able to plan and facilitate the employee's return to the workplace, where necessary, in order to help him/her to re-join the organisation successfully.

EAP SERVICES

An EAP policy can make mention of the core services offered by the organisation. EAP core services[371] should:

- identify, take in, refer and provide care;
- provide web-based education and self-help materials;

- refer employees to human resource management;
- train employees and provide leadership;
- consult with the human resource manager on employee performance issues;
- monitor/manage case and follow-up services;
- promote EAP services to employees and families;
- analyse and report data on the effects of the EAP on the organisation;
- evaluate employees' fitness for duty;
- manage critical incident stress;
- consult on workplace violence;
- support work-life balance;
- provide counsel on financial/legal issues;
- promote workplace wellness and health;
- offer regulatory compliance services;
- plan for work return (after disabled or family medical leave); and
- provide on-site wellness events (biometric screenings, health fairs etc.).

An EAP needs a clear statement of policy and service principles, which should include the intentions, procedures and available services in the programme, in order to clarify the duties, rights, responsibilities and privileges of all involved (i.e., management, programme staff, employees and the unions).[372] Designing a clear EAP policy also helps in creating stability and a high morale in the workplace by attending to employees' wellbeing. This, coupled with a high-performing caring culture, ensures the employability of employees.[373] In relation to the above, the following are EAP service policy principles that can also be included:[374]

1. ***Equality:*** the programme services are for all employees (permanent and contracted), regardless of their rank or position. All employees must be treated equally.
2. ***Confidentiality and privacy:*** professional confidentiality is respected and the programme will strive towards service provision in an atmosphere of privacy and trust. Confidentiality and privacy are discussed in more detail in the next chapter under Confidentiality and the Protection of Personal Information Act.
3. ***Dignity and respect:*** programme services will be provided courteously, with dignity and respect.
4. ***Promptness of the service:*** within practical realities, the interventions of the programme should be timely.

5. ***Information disclosure and misuse:*** information obtained within the confines of professional helping processes, such as in counselling, problem-solving and dispute resolution, will not be used or disclosed without the permission of the persons concerned.
6. ***Accessibility of programme services:*** accessibility of the services will be ensured within the bounds of practicality.
7. ***Voluntary participation:*** programme services are provided on the basis of the willing participation of employees. Situations of mandatory referral will also be treated on the same basis of willingness to accept programme services.
8. ***Non-victimisation:*** employees who participate in programme activities will not be victimised. Participation in the programme activities should not have a bearing on an employee's job security, promotion or future prospects.
9. ***Instrument of punishment:*** even though referrals and professional recommendations of the programme staff will be required by the employer, taking part in the programme services should not be used as disciplinary measure. Programme services are to be utilised in the spirit of an effort to remedy problematic situations. The programme is not to/should not be used as an instrument of punishment.
10. ***Professional service:*** professional programme services have to be rendered by qualified personnel. The programme and professional staff will assume a posture of non-interference in employer-employee relations.

Beidel and Brennan[375] suggested that the EAP core services are:

- consultation with, training of, and assistance to the organisational leadership (managers, supervisors, and union stewards) who are seeking to manage the troubled employee, enhance the work environment, and improve employee job performance; and outreach to and education of employees and their family members about the availability of EAP services;
- confidential and timely problem identification/assessment services for employee clients with personal concerns that may affect their job performance;
- the use of constructive confrontation, motivation, and short-term interventions with employee clients to address problems that affect job performance;
- the referral of employees for diagnosis, treatment and assistance, including case monitoring and follow-up service;
- consultation with work organisations about establishing and maintaining effective relations with treatment and other service providers, and about managing provider contracts;
- consultation with work organisations to encourage the availability of, and employee access to, health benefits covering medical and behavioural problems, including but not limited to alcoholism, drug abuse, and mental and emotional disorders; and

- identification of the effects of EAP services on the work organisation and individual job performance.

The Integrated Model of Occupational Assistance considers EAP services as focusing on:[376]

- physical health: physical fitness, nutrition, adequate rest and sleep and medical self-care, which includes the absence of disease as well as behaviour that affects biological functioning (smoking and drug use);
- emotional or psychological health: the ability to maintain a relative amount of control over emotional states in response to life events, stress management, and appropriate responses to emotional crises;
- social health: with regard to family, work, school, religious affiliations, social values, customs, and social support, social health is the ability to interact effectively with others, which includes the development of appropriate relationships with friends, families, co-workers and communities;
- intellectual health: encompasses education, achievement, role fulfilment and career development, and the ability to engage in clear thinking and to think independently and critically; and
- spiritual health: love, charity, purpose, inner peace, caring for others, prayer and the connection to a larger purpose other than oneself or one's immediate social circle.

CONCLUSION

This chapter presented a myriad of EAP services offered by practitioners in their organisations. It is the responsibility of the HR department to determine the services and processes of EAP service delivery that should be included in the policy document. The provision of services should be supported by the organisation's capacity to provide human and financial resources.

Chapter 9

THE ROLE, FUNCTION AND ETHICAL PRINCIPLES OF THE PROFESSIONAL TEAM

EAP professionals are guided by the Code of Ethics of the Employee Assistance Professionals Association (EAPA), which provides guidance with regard to how they should conduct themselves. The Code clearly defines acceptable standards of behaviour for the benefit of the client (employees, employers, unions, colleagues, other professionals, the community and society). When organisations process any personal information about their employees then the Protection of Personal Information Act (2013), which will be discussed in this chapter, applies.

Professional organisations for mental health practitioners such as psychiatrists, psychologists, social workers, mental health counsellors, pastoral counsellors, and psychiatric nurses have all developed codes of ethics that describe appropriate behaviour for therapists.[377] Both internal and external service providers and practitioners have to be ethical in their conduct.

A detailed discussion of ethical considerations for EAP implementation was presented in previous chapters. Please refer to this chapter for ethical aspects that have to be included in an EAP policy.

The following is an overview of the ethical codes of service providers and practitioners that are relevant for an EAP policy (EAPA-SA Code of Ethics).

Public responsibility

In terms of public responsibility, EAP practitioners are expected to conduct themselves as follows:

- The EAPA-SA Board, Regional Chapters and all EAPA-SA members are responsible for educating and fostering professional development.
- EAPA-SA members are encouraged to create and maintain the highest standards in their profession and promote EAPs to the public.
- EAPA-SA members shall conduct themselves in their professional activities in a way that does not denigrate other professionals for the sake of promoting their own interests. They shall also conduct themselves in a manner that does not undermine public confidence in their ability, or that of other professionals, to carry out their professional duties.
- Co-operation in a professional community precludes fraudulent or misleading advertising practices, and requires that professional qualifications be presented to the public in an accurate and truthful manner.

- EAPA-SA members shall bring allegations of misconduct by a professional colleague to the attention of those charged with the responsibility of investigating them, doing so without malice and with no breaches of confidentiality other than those necessary for the proper investigatory process. Members who are themselves the subject of allegations shall provide all reasonable assistance to aid EAPA-SA in the investigatory process which may, but will not necessarily, result in bringing the matter to the attention of the relevant statutory body.
- Research shall be conducted in accordance with the ethical standards set out in the EAPA-SA Standards.

Confidentiality and the Protection of Personal Information Act

Confidentiality as an ethical responsibility suggests that:

- EAPA-SA members shall regard all client-related information as confidential and the release of information will only be done in compliance with a court order, a subpoena, or with the written permission and consent of the client;
- EAPA-SA members shall inform clients fully about their rights regarding the scope and limitations of confidential communications;
- EAPA-SA members shall not convey personally identifiable information obtained in the course of professional work, except when working in a team (or with professional supervision) and if such disclosure might be in the client's own interests. Members must make clear to clients the extent to which personal information may be shared between colleagues;
- in exceptional circumstances, where there is sufficient evidence to raise serious concern about the physical wellbeing and safety of the client, or about others who may be threatened by the client (and after consulting with a senior colleague or professional supervisor/case manager), members shall take such steps as are judged necessary to inform appropriate third parties without prior consent. Such disclosure may, on rare occasions, be required by law, for instance in the case of physical child abuse; and
- "client" shall include individual employees or members of their families as well as the employer, company, organisation or public institution. Members shall also regard their organisational consulting activities as confidential, unless written permission has been obtained to do otherwise by the company or organisation.

If organisations process any personal information of their employees, then the Protection of Personal Information Act (2013) applies. The objective of this Act (the PoPI Act, for short) is to put measures in place to protect the privacy of South African citizens.[378] The conditions of the PoPI Act relate to ethical values in the processing of personal information. It makes good business sense to implement privacy principles as part of any EAP process, to protect the participants and to ensure that the data are only used for the purposes intended. The Protection of Personal Information Act of 2013 regulates the processing of personal information as required by the Constitution of the Republic of South Africa (1996), which provides everyone with the right to privacy. This right provides "protection against the unlawful collection, retention, dissemination and use of personal information; with the objective of promoting the protection of personal information".[379] This personal information does not only relate to the participant's name, surname, age, gender, race, contact information or residential information, but also includes information pertaining to their wellbeing, opinions, views and preferences, which is often collected as part of the information needed to manage an EAP effectively.

The PoPI Act defines personal information as follows:

"(P)ersonal information means information relating to an identifiable, living, natural person, and where it is applicable, an identifiable, existing juristic person, including, but not limited to:

- information relating to the race, gender, sex, pregnancy, marital status, national, ethnic or social origin, colour, sexual orientation, age, physical or mental health, wellbeing, disability, religion, conscience, belief, culture, language and birth of the person;
- information relating to the education or the medical, financial, criminal or employment history of the person;
- any identifying number, symbol, e-mail address, physical address, telephone number, location information, online identifier or other particular assignment to the person;
- the biometric information of the person;
- the personal opinions, views or preferences of the person;
- correspondence sent by the person that is implicitly or explicitly of a private or confidential nature or further correspondence that would reveal the contents of the original correspondence;
- the views or opinions of another individual about the person; and
- the name of the person if it appears with other personal information relating to the person or if the disclosure of the name itself would reveal information about the person."[380]

It is the responsibility of the practitioners and service providers to establish the risk of personal information exposure and to implement the necessary controls to prevent such exposure and to preserve confidentiality and uphold the right to privacy.

Professional competence

Competency to practice and to help clients with many different issues is an essential requirement and many ethical dilemmas may occur in such practice. Sharf[381] pointed out that difficult issues, such as the need to protect people a client intends to harm, have been given much attention and have complex solutions. Practitioners and services providers have the following responsibilities:

1. EAPA-SA and all its members who are EAP practitioners are expected to be proficient in the knowledge of work organisations, EAP policy and administration, and direct services. They support and work towards the professional standards published by the EAPA-SA branch.
2. EAPA-SA members recognise the boundaries of their own competence and do not attempt to provide services for which they do not have the appropriate preparation or specialist qualifications.
3. EAPA-SA members take all reasonable steps to ensure that their qualifications or capabilities are not misrepresented by others and to correct any such misrepresentation. EAPA-SA members refrain from practice when their physical, emotional or psychological condition, whether as a result of alcohol, drugs, illness, personal stress or another condition, would impair their abilities and/or professional judgment.

These ethical codes are in substantial agreement about actions that constitute ethical and unethical behaviour on the part of the practitioner, hence all practitioners should accept their profession's ethical codes.[382]

EAPA-SA members who are in violation of the Association's code are subject to termination of membership or other appropriate action if they:

- are expelled from or disciplined by other professional organisations;
- are disciplined by professional regulatory bodies;
- fail to co-operate at any point from the inception of an ethical complaint through the proceedings of that complaint;
- receive a conviction for criminal behaviour arising from their professional work; or
- engage in conduct which could lead to a conviction relating to their professional work.

Record-keeping

Employees' and organisational EAP records are confidential, thus the following is expected of practitioners:

1. EAPA-SA's Standards for EAPs pertaining to confidentiality and record-keeping must be followed in the generation, transmission, storage and disposal of client records.
2. Client records should contain only information that is directly related to and necessary for the provision of service. Any record should be taken down on an informed client basis.
3. Information in a client's record is privileged and must be maintained in a confidential and professional manner. Each entry should be accurate, timely, complete and related directly to services to the client. EAPA-SA members must be mindful of the potential effect of client information kept on record. This information will be secured under lock and key and kept separate from other files. All records are to be kept for a minimum of six (6) years after the closure of a case, or as dictated by South African law. After the minimum time has passed, the client files should be destroyed or archived.
4. The information should be accurate and free from speculation or value judgements about the client, the work organisation or others.
5. The information contained in the records should be disclosed only with the client's consent and only to those named in the written consent.
6. It is considered best practice to allow clients to view their own records if this is requested. EAPA-SA members must take all reasonable steps to safeguard the security of any records they take down, including those on computer. Where they have limited control over access to the records they draw up, discretion must be exercised over the information entered on the records, particularly identifying information.
7. The disposal of records must be undertaken in a manner that ensures complete confidentiality, as required by professional standards and law.

Client protection

With regard to client protection during service delivery:

1. EAPA-SA members must naturally operate within the Constitution of the Republic of South Africa with regard to non-discrimination, as outlined in the Employment Equity Act of 1998 as well as the Protection of Personal Information Act (2013). All research should conform to national and international standards in that it should safeguard the welfare of the research participants. If an organisation is found guilty of an offence against the PoPI Act it can result in penalties such as a fine or imprisonment up to ten years, as well as administrative fines not exceeding R10 million.

   Various professional bodies in South Africa have ethical codes that can provide guidance to practitioners, researchers or consultants. The South African Board for People Practices has core ethical values that human resource practitioners should uphold, as well as a code of conduct. Similarly, the Health Professions Council of South Africa (HPCSA) has Ethical

Rules of Conduct, while members of the Information Systems Audit and Control Association (ISACA) for audit professionals in information technology have to conform to their Code of Professional Ethics (2016). Furthermore, the Human Sciences Research Council (HSRC) has published a Code of Research Ethics, which gives guidelines for research projects in their domain and serves as a sound guideline for organisations engaged in research.[383]

2. Members should not give or receive financial consideration for referring clients to particular therapists or treatment programmes.

Hiring

In terms of appointments for the EAP, it is the responsibility of practitioners to do the following:

1. EAPA-SA members should strive to abide by the principle of equal treatment for all. They must take all reasonable steps to promote equality of opportunity in all aspects of the provision of EAP services.
2. EAPA-SA members shall not discriminate when employing persons and shall act in accordance with the Constitution of the Republic of South Africa, as outlined in the Employment Equity Act of 1998.
3. All policies and procedures pertaining to employment should be reviewed to ensure compliance with the stated equal opportunities policy and current legislation.
4. When contracting or sub-contracting services, EAP professionals shall ensure that the contractor has, and abides by, an equal opportunities policy.

Business practices

EAP services are provided in a business environment, hence it is critical that:

1. EAPA-SA members believe in the fair use and encouragement of competition. EAPA-SA encourages all types of fair and reasonable competition between different programmes for the same end use;
2. EAPA-SA members will conduct supplier/vendor relationships so that there are no personal obligations, actual or implied, which might affect business decisions in awarding the business; and
3. EAPA-SA members must consider their professional conduct relating to the business of their EAP. Although some areas may not apply to certain EAP models, EAP professionals must avoid fraudulent or misleading practices in representation, sales, competition, advertising, and all general business practices and operations.

Members must minimally expect that their professional conduct will not harm others, both in the field and in the community. EAPA-SA members should strive to:

- exert their positions, but not at the expense of others;
- conduct themselves fairly, and their service must be delivered as agreed to;
- contribute to the betterment of others in the field;
- protect the anonymity and confidentiality of clients; and
- conduct themselves in a manner which maintains and enhances the image and integrity of professional EAP provision.

Complaints procedure

Under the terms of the EAPA-SA Code of Ethics, the Board (or any Chapter) is required to investigate complaints about EAPA-SA and Chapter members. The following process is adopted for complaints processing:

1. All complaints in South Africa will be brought before the nearest Chapter Executive Committee, unless a conflict of interest exists prohibiting the processing of the complaint. In these circumstances, the complaint may be passed to the Executive Committee of the EAPA-SA Board.
2. When the Executive Committee reaches finality on a complaint, the matter is closed. The complainant or respondent may appeal that decision, in the first instance, to the EAPA-SA Board Executive, and thereafter to the EAPA-SA Board. All appeals will be based only on the information provided initially to the Board's Executive Committee – appeals will not involve a new investigation or hearing. The EAPA Ethics Committee in the USA is the last appeal and will make the final decisions (subject to approval by the EAPA Board of Directors in the USA).
3. When a complaint is processed by the EAPA Ethics Committee in the USA, any appeal will be directed to the EAPA Board of Directors.

The investigatory procedure involves the following:

1. Any complaint that is made must be in writing and must be submitted to the Chapter Chairperson.
2. Upon receipt of the complaint, the Chairperson shall nominate a senior and experienced member of the Chapter to conduct an initial investigation. The purpose of this investigation will be to determine whether the allegation is justified. The investigating officer will provide the respondent with the complaint letter and invite a written response within thirty (30) days.

3. If the investigating officer decides that the complaint must be investigated, the Chapter Chairperson will appoint the Chairperson of the Disciplinary Committee. Together they will form a panel of a minimum of four (4) and not more than six (6) members. One of these will be the investigating officer and the other, the Chairperson of the Committee.
4. Although the EAPA-SA President may not be a member of the Disciplinary Committee, it is his/her responsibility to ensure that no member of the Committee has a conflict of interest in the investigation.

A disciplinary investigation is conducted as follows:

- The investigating officer will present to the Committee such information as is available and relevant. The complainant and the respondent will both be invited to separate parts of the hearing and are allowed to present further evidence in writing if they wish. The respondent may be accompanied at the hearing by one other person.
- It is the responsibility of the Disciplinary Committee to decide whether or not the respondent is guilty of professional misconduct under the EAPA-SA Code of Ethics, or the EAPA-SA Constitution.
- All investigations are to be conducted in such a way as to eliminate any negligence in the review process; breach of confidentiality; conflict of interest; and/or defamation (libel/slander).

If the Disciplinary Committee finds someone guilty, one or more of the following actions may be taken:

- The member may be reprimanded or severely reprimanded.
- The member may be requested to give an undertaking to refrain from continuing or repeating the offending conduct.
- The member may be suspended from EAPA-SA for no more than two (2) years.
- The member may be suspended from EAPA Inc. for no more than two (2) years.
- The member may be expelled from EAPA-SA or EAPA Inc. or both.

All disciplinary matters should be dealt with in a constructive and conciliatory manner, rather than following a punitive approach.

CONCLUSION

EAPA-SA provides guidelines of ethical codes governing the conduct of professionals in the field. These codes can be used by providing a summary in an EAP policy, indicating to employees and the organisation what to expect with regard to professional team conduct.

Chapter 10

QUALITY MANAGEMENT OF EAPs

Adherence to professional standards and guidelines ensures viable EAPs. The purpose of non-regulatory guidelines is to assist all relevant stakeholders to establish quality EAPs in accordance with international best practices and enhance existing EAPs.[384]

EAPs need oversight to ensure that services to recipients are not compromised and to enhance their credibility in organisations. The Standards for Employee Assistance Programmes in South Africa were developed in 1999 by the Employee Assistance Professionals Association – South African Chapter (EAPA-SA), and revised in 2005 as guidelines for the implementation of EAPs. The 27 standards represent not only the national agreed level of professional best practice for EAPs, but also outline the basic principles that these programmes should adhere to and the key elements they should contain.

The function of an EAP Quality Assurance Committee

The appointment of a Quality Assurance Committee is essential to ensure quality service delivery. This Committee is the formal mobilisation of the support necessary for an EAP and its services to become known, needed, trusted and accepted throughout a corporation, organisation or union.[385]

The key responsibilities and tasks of an EAP Quality Assurance Committee are to:

- review established guidelines to ensure agreement and understanding of rules and procedures;
- develop and implement changes in guidelines when necessary and receive input from interested parties;
- develop and implement strategies in conjunction with a coordinator to ensure that employees are aware of the employee assistance programme; and
- be involved in the evaluation of the programme.

In addition to the above, Govender[386] argued that a Quality Assurance Committee can be expected to fulfil the following functions:

- Provide programme support and legitimacy.
- Act as a resource of information – organisational profiling and needs assessment.

- Ensure linkages with all relevant stakeholders.
- Be involved with programme design – give advice on policy, goals, objectives, implementation plans and procedures, programme services, as well as marketing.
- Evaluate and give critical feedback on programme initiatives.
- Conduct ongoing reviews of operations.
- Support EAP confidentiality safeguards.

A Quality Assurance Committee acts as an advisory committee and consists of representatives from labour, management, personnel, labour relations, medical personnel and others within the organisation. Govender[387] indicated that all relevant role players in an organisation should contribute to and participate in the effective design and operation of an EAP. Their combined expertise will help shape the EAP and, in doing so, a degree of ownership of the EAP will come about that can assist the development of the model in its quest for legitimacy.

The process of formulating EAP quality standards for internal and external service providers and practitioners

Although the application of the standard criteria will ensure the creation of quality EAPs, these guidelines should not inhibit the opportunity for organisations to develop customised employee assistance models.[388] Whether the organisation chooses an internal or external model, the EAP services should be well implemented and well suited to the organisation. In order to produce a positive and successful EAP, the organisation should consider a policy guideline.

The organisation's policy should include the following core ingredients/quality standards of a successful EAP:[389]

- Accessibility.
- Training for managers and supervisors.
- Management orientation.
- Insurance coverage.
- Broad service components, which cover all/various employee problems.
- Professional leadership.
- Programme evaluation and follow-up.
- Confidentiality and anonymity.

There are a variety of ways in which standards can be implemented. When designing, implementing or evaluating an EAP, each organisation should apply these standards and guidelines based on its own unique organisational culture and operations.[390]

QUALITY ASSURANCE MEASURES AND STANDARDS

A "standard" is defined in the Oxford English Dictionary as a required, expected or accepted level of quality. It is also described as a specified level of proficiency. Quality is measured against standards.

For an organisation wishing to implement an EAP, the standards document provides a very good framework of best practice. According to EAPA-SA,[391] the quality assurance of an EAP is based on the agreed level of best practice or description of the ideal situation. Credibility and quality assurance for EAPs is best achieved by practitioners adhering to stipulated ethical guidelines.[392]

An organisation can ensure quality by putting the following measures in place:

1. ***Staffing:*** employers can ensure that their employees have access to quality EAP services provided by experienced, formally trained, professional practitioners who are meticulous about maintaining confidentiality. This results in high utilisation of the EAP, directly profiting the employer by providing cost savings and limiting legal exposure. EAP practitioners have a potentially profound effect on their clients and, via consultation and case management, clients are assured of authentic, quality services.
2. ***Training and development:*** it is important to enhance the skills of the EAP team. Practitioners' professional proficiency is a quality standard that is crucial to creating and sustaining a successful EAP. Allocating trained personnel with the right degree of expertise to fulfil multiple roles in running the EAP will ensure the legitimacy of the programme, client satisfaction and customised services that will not only add value to the lives of employees, but also enhance overall organisational functioning. EAP practitioners need to possess comprehensive knowledge and be proficient in dealing with the diagnosis and treatment of work dysfunctions. This includes expertise in marriage and family counselling and general emotional problems, as well as other typical problems such as financial and legal troubles, and conducting basic unbiased interviews.

Training is an essential feature of a successful EAP; it helps bring about changes in existing levels of knowledge and attitudes that enable EAP practitioners to realise the objectives of the programme within the organisation. Training is also a powerful tool to strengthen communication, eliminate misconceptions and introduce change. Govender[393] stated that without proper training and regular re-training, supervisors, personnel administrators and other contributors to the programme would fail to pool their resources toward developing an effective EAP and utilising its services optimally.

This training also includes continuous professional development. EAPA-SA[394] requires that EAP professionals maintain and upgrade their knowledge by belonging to an organisation specifically designed for EAP professionals, by attending training and/or professional development programmes, and by maintaining regular ongoing contact with other EAP professionals. The goal of this standard is to enhance the knowledge, skills and attitudes of EAP professionals and to ensure that they remain aware of new developments and technologies in EAP service delivery.

Management and leadership: professional management and leadership provided by a skilled professional who has credibility in the eyes of the employees is a critical attribute of quality assurance and a successful EAP. Such a manager(s) should be well trained in the nature of EAP services in order to provide value to the programme and the organisation. Effective management and leadership will ensure that managers, supervisors and shop stewards are familiar with, understand the dimensions of, and are prepared to fully engage with, the supervisory referral process and the dynamic EAP consultation process.[395] It will be a vehicle and framework for strategic partnerships between the EAP professional and any other key stakeholder within the organisation.

Mogorosi[396] suggested that leadership training contributes to EAP quality through:

- its emphasis on management's support of the programme;
- the explanation of supervisors' roles in the implementation of the programme; and
- a demonstration of how programmes can be helpful to supervisors and managers in their job responsibilities.

Record-keeping: record-keeping enables the EAP Quality Assurance Committee to design and evaluate EAPs in that records are kept of the clients' demographics and profiles of problems for the purposes of identifying trends. This informs the planning of primary and secondary prevention programmes. Records also aid in monitoring the utilisation of the programme and referral sources.[397] EAPA-SA[398] indicates that the record-keeping system needs to capture and maintain records on administrative matters, meetings, clinical information, corporate client information, evaluation data, marketing and promotional material, as well as training material, in order to ensure quality and continuity of care.

CONCLUSION

Quality assurance and management is mainly concerned with ensuring best practice in EAPs, as employees and their next of kin will only use EAPs that they trust and find credible. It is important to have a system that can be applied in an organisation to enhance the quality assurance of EAPs. Such a system will require the establishment of an EAP Quality Assurance Committee to develop standards and measures.

Chapter 11

EAP IMPACT ASSESSMENT

This chapter outlines the importance of an impact assessment in EAPs and the process that could be followed.

The value of impact assessments or the evaluation of EAPs

The way in which organisations evaluate their EAPs and what they consider a success will be related to their reasons for commencing with them in the first place. From a research perspective, one of the most fluctuating aspects of EAP evaluation is the measurement of indirect results. When a person who has been relieved of a considerable psychological burden returns to work with a degree of constructive energy and commitment, how is this measured quantitatively and qualitatively? However, it is important to evaluate an EAP to justify its existence to an external authority, to ascertain the extent to which the EAP is reaching its goals, and to find ways to improve its effectiveness.

The goals of an EAP service should be established from the beginning in order for organisations to evaluate whether the goals are being met or not. Organisations rely on the premise that effective EAPs do assist troubled employees, and as a consequence ultimately help the organisation and pay for themselves. Outcome evaluation is necessary to ensure that an EAP is correctly designed for the organisation in which it is operating, and to ensure that it meets the needs of the employees and the organisation.[399] According to Govender,[400] failure to monitor the progress or impact of an intervention can result in serious gaps in the case management process and can prolong the time it may take to assist a client. It also has a negative impact on the partnership between the EAP practitioner, the supervisor/union representative and the client, and might therefore have an adverse effect on the effectiveness of the intervention as a whole.

While an evaluation might demonstrate the overall effectiveness of an EAP, there may still exist benefit inequity, indicating that "effectiveness is undesirably varied among different groups of employees".[401] Hence a better understanding of benefit equity in outcomes among EAP users is relevant to both EAP providers and purchasers. In the EAP field, "benefit equity" has been broadly defined as the equitable distribution of benefits among the different groups of workers covered by and accessing an EAP.[402]

According to Milot,[403] the purposes of evaluating benefit equity are as follows:

- An evaluation of benefit equity helps determine whether inequities exists in "EAP care" between different types of covered employees.

- For the providers of EAP, the integration of benefit equity analyses into routine evaluations could identify groups of employees benefitting less than others.
- This then provides an opportunity to improve practices and the delivery of services to those kinds of users.

Impact analysis focuses on an examination of a programme to determine whether the programme activities are changing any activity targeted, and whether it is achieving long-lasting positive results.[404] The most popular metrics for measuring EAP impact are user satisfaction surveys, first-hand accounts of employees' experiences, and published studies, however these methods have their shortcomings. Simple user satisfaction surveys involve a number of variables that can have an impact on the results of a survey, such as whether the EAP provider is likable or not, or how many employees actually complete the survey. Published studies, in turn, validate approaches rather than specific programmes, which implies that a certain study may prove that a certain method works, but does not guarantee that any EAP service provider can reproduce the same results when using the same method.

Employers should not be asking whether EAPs are effective, but rather which specific EAP service providers are effective. Unless a business can link the outcomes of an EAP to positive outcomes in the workplace, the business may not invest in an EAP. Businesses should evaluate their EAP provider on five key elements that affect workplace functioning: presentism, absenteeism, life satisfaction, work engagement and workplace distress.

Monitoring and evaluation strategies of EAP services at an individual, group and organisational level

Organisations need to know that the EAP is running smoothly and that the efficiency and quality of the service is high. ***Evaluation*** is the identification of the effects of EAP services on the work organisation and individual job performance.[405] Establishing mechanisms and processes for evaluating the effect of EAPs is a critical research endeavour,[406] however even though such a process of evaluation is an essential basis for the continued improvement and development of a service, it does not measure whether the EAP service is "value for money" or whether the EAP is designed effectively and appropriately.

Mogorosi[407] argued that programme evaluation is a significant component of EAPs, noting that this evaluation follows different paths and formats as it is informed by the reasons for the assessment of a specific programme. An evaluation process can address misconceptions and misunderstandings that can lead to unrealistic expectations of EAP service delivery and the benefits that organisations can expect from having an EAP.[408] Evaluation is often neglected because practitioners may not feel competent or confident to pursue this area of practice, or believe that evaluation should be done only after the programme is fully established. Identifying the purpose and objectives of EAPs and the ways EAPs are used in modern organisations is critical in framing the focus, design and analyses of EAP evaluations.[409]

There are two main forms of evaluations. Firstly, evaluation can be in the form of ***process evaluation***, which is aimed at ensuring that programme agreements, policies and procedures are adhered to.

Mogorosi[410] indicated that stipulated procedures, steps and stages, are checked to ascertain whether they are being properly followed as stipulated. Process evaluation involves the following:

- ***A service audit:*** the service audit focuses on a range of variables including age, gender, marital status, educational history, occupation, ethnic origin, geographic location, socio-demographic information, as well as information of a psychological nature (e.g. what the range of problems is). This type of data is beneficial in identifying specific needs in the service delivery.
- ***Quality assurance:*** this is concerned primarily with the process of providing counselling, and involves the setting and monitoring of "performance standards". Monitoring the quality of the actual counselling and the quality of the service is a key issue.

The second form of evaluation is ***outcome evaluation***, where the aims, goals and procedures as stipulated in programme policy documents and manuals are assessed.[411] The purpose of outcome evaluation is to establish whether set goals, over a given time frame, are being achieved. Although organisations conduct process evaluations, this type of evaluation on its own is sometimes enough, as EAPs rely on the assumption that well-run EAPs do assist staff in distress and, as a result, help organisations and profit them in the long term. Yet this assumption should not be made automatically as the context in every organisation is different. The "whole service" should be evaluated in order to prove that the assumption is valid in the particular organisation. The evaluation may range from simple tabulation of employees' programme participation, to their solicitation of the services, utilisation of the services, satisfaction with the services rendered, and demonstration of the degree of popularity of the services or programme components among employees.[412] Evaluation must focus on:

- ***implementation:*** to measure how well the programme is operating;
- ***utilisation:*** to measure how well the programme is utilised; and
- ***effectiveness:*** to measure how well the output and objectives of the organisation have been achieved.

Baseline indicators for a successful EAP should be determined when the EAP is initiated, so that once the programme is established, there will be predetermined factors to measure it against.[413] Mogorosi[414] suggested that process and outcome evaluations should be conducted against the criteria in Table 11.1.

Table 11.1: EAP evaluation citation elements[415]

Elements of process and outcome evaluation	
Measures of work performance	Employee rate of absenteeism. Number of disciplinary actions received. Number of employee grievances filed. Number of on-the-job accidents. Number of employee visits to the medical unit. Amount of employees' compensation claims. Amount of sickness and accident claims paid.
Elements of programme evaluation	Policies and procedures. Training of frontline supervisors. Programme services. Follow-up work.
Six major criteria	Confidentiality. Accidents. Staff expertise and availability. Flexibility. Accountability. Cost-effectiveness.
Elements of programme evaluation	Health and attitudes of employees. Absenteeism and productivity. Cost-effectiveness. Reduction in grievances.
Evaluation of an EAP	Programme utilisation. Programme penetration. Referral sources. Employees' awareness of the programme. Programme adequacy. Compliance assessment. Programme efforts. Programme effectiveness. Programme equity. Client satisfaction.

Therefore, in addition to process evaluation (quality and efficiency), outcome evaluation is required to ensure that the EAP is correctly designed for the particular organisation in which it is operating, and that it is meeting the needs of that organisation and its employees. Outcome evaluation should include an analysis of the organisation's "bottom line" personnel data such as absence due to illness and unwanted staff turnover, because it is necessary to be able to establish the link between counselling employees and personnel performance.

In terms of assessment activities, the following can be included in the process of outcome evaluations:[416]

Effectiveness: this usually addresses the issue of whether employees who receive treatment improve. Milot[417] maintained that, at an individual level, the measure of outcome/benefit is the degree of problem resolution reported by an employee at the end of a service provided by an EAP practitioner. Pre- and post-counselling comparison is one way to evaluate effectiveness, by showing that a change has occurred following counselling. However, this method is not without its limitations as change cannot be attributed solely to counselling, because counselling is not the only thing which is taking place in the employee's life, and there could be other major influences which may account for the change. In order to address this challenge, a proper control group would be required. Programme activities are assessed to establish whether the activities are the best way to address the stipulated needs of the employees.

Programme evaluation is a tool that helps programme funders, organisations and programme staff to assess whether the appropriate services are being offered and set programme goals are being met, and it provides guidance on how to revise the programme in the future.[418] If the EAP is not perceived as a viable and available support for staff, it is not possible to assess how effective it is in improving individual and organisational outcomes.[419] According to Sieberhagen, Pienaar and Els,[420] items that can be used by organisations to measure the effectiveness of EAPs include the following:

- Utilisation rate.
- Absenteeism.
- Feedback from staff.
- HIV registration rate.
- Number of HIV+ employees that return to work.
- Medical boarding rate.
- Success of smoking cessation.
- Extent of marketing.
- Number of employees reached.

- Psychological wellness of employees.
- Chronic disease reports from the medical aid.
- Problems with reports from service providers.
- Buy-in.
- Targeted projects focused on real needs.
- Good planning.
- Looking at different indicators.
- Exit interviews.
- Reduction in number of suicides.

The utilisation rate is an important aspect of evaluating and monitoring a programme. During the evaluation of an EAP, utilisation can be measured by asking if employees used the wellness programme, and what services they utilised.[421] Examining variations in the utilisation of different services and constraints in service delivery can reveal nuances in EAP usage, aspects of risk management and shortfalls in EAP offerings, thereby enhancing the potential to effectively meet the terms of workplace psychological contracts.[422]

Cost-benefit analysis: this activity aims to evaluate the costs and benefits solely in monetary terms. However, the validity of converting psychological outcomes into monetary terms comes into question. It is beneficial to distinguish between "hard" and "soft" data. Hard data (absence and performance) tend to be quantifiable, whereas soft data (client self-reporting measures, both quantitative and qualitative) are less easy to verify independently. Third-party sources can be used for verification purposes so that reliance is not placed entirely on the client's perspective. In a review of 32 health promotion programme evaluations, it was found that 28 programmes reported medical cost savings,[423] thus EAPs have been successful in reducing employee healthcare costs.

Cost-efficiency: this process involves comparing two or more interventions in terms of the cost of achieving a specific outcome, such as getting an individual back to work. The focus is on whether the programme is reaching its set goals, using the best possible ways and means. The main question is whether whatever is being done gives the best value for the resources put into it; it is about programme costs.

The aim then is to establish which intervention achieves the best therapeutic results in relation to the cost of implementation. In the event of diminishing returns, as the number of counselling sessions continue, decisions have to be made as to how limited resources can best be utilised to achieve the maximum therapeutic benefit for employees at work. Evaluation techniques include:

- data analysis of the utilisation and productivity of the EAP service;
- surveys, including client feedback (evaluation), client progress questionnaires and surveys on the effectiveness of EAP training; and
- interviews with clients.

Exploring the processes that EAP providers use to evaluate their own service delivery, teasing out the differences between EAP providers, as well as the impact of the types of EAP services and the requirements of the organisations being serviced, can be helpful in improving the current practices in an organisation.[424]

EAP EVALUATION AND MONITORING TOOLS

In most organisations, monitoring is the most neglected function within an EAP. Closer monitoring of outcomes can mean a more proactive and prompt approach to intervention, enhancing the probability of improved outcomes.[425] A well-defined mechanism for case monitoring is essential to monitor the progress of treatment parallel to work performance, and to identify relapse and recidivism.[426]

Focus groups can be used to evaluate EAPs, where a group of participants can indicate the programmes' strengths and weaknesses. Evidence-based evaluation of EAP effectiveness is critical to demonstrate an improvement in employees' psychological functioning and performance.[427] The value of focus groups is that group processes can help participants to explore and clarify their views in a manner that would not always be possible in a survey. If a focus group is conducted with different language groups, the language proficiency of the facilitator is very important; the facilitator should be familiar with the language of the group and should be able to conduct the focus group in the mother tongue of the participants. This usually ensures better understanding and participation in the process.[428]

The impact assessment of EAPs can be made by means of ***interviews*** about the efficacy of EAPs in providing information and counselling services, and to identify the scope of EAPs within the organisations. The value of interviews lies in that they are very flexible; various types of face-to-face interviews can be used. It is important that the interviewer select the appropriate type of interview, which will ensure that a rapport is established.

The interviewer or facilitator must be competent and trained to conduct interviews and focus groups according to the guidelines for quantitative research, to ensure the trustworthiness of the data. The aim of collecting and disseminating the information is to empower organisations to strengthen their programmes.

An EAP ***satisfaction survey study*** can be used to collect uniform and standardised data that will allow for a comparison of EAPs' services on an annual basis. Evaluation, in this instance, is the systematic and objective assessment of an ongoing or completed project, programme or policy, its design and its implementation. It is the comparison of the actual project/activities against agreed strategic plans, and looks at what the programme has set out to do and what it has accomplished. Such a survey can evaluate the following:[429]

- What the programme has set out to do: this entails the goal that the EAP section has set for itself, for example reducing absenteeism by 20%.
- What has been accomplished: this focuses primarily on the achievements in relation to the goals that have been set, for example, did the EAP manage to reduce absenteeism by 20%?
- How the EAP has accomplished its goals: this entails the approach, method and strategies employed to reach the goals and establish an effective programme.

Surveys can provide ***primary data***, which are obtained by means of a questionnaire based on the minimum standards issued by an organisation to monitor progress of the implementation of the EAP policy framework. This helps to determine the efficacy of the EAP in providing counselling, support and other services to employees. ***Secondary data*** focus on the issues relevant to EAPs and their roles in dealing with employee dysfunctions in organisations.

The same applies to data analysis and the reporting of impact analysis results or findings. This process involves a ***gap analysis*** of EAPs, with the objective of investigating the implementation of EAPs within organisations. A gap analysis is conducted to establish how effective EAPs are and to what extent such EAPs have been implemented and are involved in employee issues in the workplace. Once the gaps have been identified, it is critical to implement continuous improvement plans to address them.

It can be challenging to objectively measure the impact of EAPs in large organisations. An example of a standardised measure to assess work performance related to the EAP and the field of Health and Productivity Management is the Health and Productivity Questionnaire (HPQ).[430] The HPQ is designed to measure the impact of chronic illness on productivity using the measures of work attendance and absenteeism, which are two important outcomes for EAPs. With norms gleaned from more than 200,000 employees worldwide, the HPQ is considered a reliable and valid measure which can be used in the workplace. A shorter and more workplace-friendly version of the HPQ, the HPQ-Select, is leading the way in corporate benchmarking in health and productivity. The HPQ-Select is administered by the Integrated Benefits Institute (IBI) and is currently being utilised by many EAPs that are working to combine their operational experiences in a large international reporting database.[431] As with any other organisational diagnosis, it is critical to only use valid and reliable measures (questionnaires). In the South African context, it is also important to ensure that the questionnaire one intends to use is valid and reliable for the specific population (for the industry or sector or race groups) in which it is intended for use.[432] The discussion of validity and reliability falls without the scope of this book, however it is critical that EAP consultants ensure that they are trained and qualified to conduct organisational diagnoses. The following book can be consulted: *Organisational Diagnosis. Tools and applications for practitioners and researchers. Editors: N. Martins, EC. Martins & R. Viljoen. Randburg: KR Publishing.*

Information collected during the monitoring and evaluations process is very useful. EAP providers may consider the information gathered to structure and market their services in a way that responds to evaluation concerns and offers reassurance of the integrity of the services being delivered.[433] (Please refer to the chapter discussing needs assessments and the use of qualitative and quantitative approaches to conduct an impact assessment or programme evaluation.)

CONCLUSION

Impact assessment and programme evaluation are important aspects of the quality assurance of EAPs. This chapter identified relevant tools for impact assessment in order to identify gaps with regard to EAP implementation in an organisation. A continuous improvement plan can be used to address the gaps or limitations of a programme.

Chapter 12

REPORT WRITING AND CONTINUOUS IMPROVEMENT PLANS FOR ALL LEVELS

Report writing is important in the process of keeping a record of the services provided to EAP service recipients in an organisation. Language is important in all reports, thus it is key that an EAP practitioner or manager should adhere to the following guidelines for a professional report:

- The report must be clear and articulate.
- Simple language that is easy to read and understand should be used.
- The report must be free of spelling and technical errors.
- The report has to be signed off by the responsible person, who in this case is the practitioner or manager.
- The report should be concise and not unnecessarily detailed.
- An editor and proof reader must have given feedback on the report.

Different templates are used by various organisations for report writing. Our approach is mainly activity-based, allowing you to determine the components that you think are relevant and should be covered in various reports.

Individual EAP reports

Individual reports are used to record the interactions between an EAP practitioner and the employee as a client.

EAP group reports

EAP practitioners are obliged to record the interactions between an EAP practitioner and the group members during their sessions.

Quality review and continuous improvement plan reports

Quality review reports are based on the findings of the EAP gap analysis, impact assessment and programme evaluation process. The findings are used to develop a continuous improvement plan with activities and deadlines.

Summary

Every organisation has its own reporting process and guidelines. It is expected of you to use your professional expertise in line with your organisational guidelines to develop templates for reporting the various activities of the EAP, in your role as a manager or practitioner.

Best practice for EAPs

Evaluation and impact assessments are conducted in order to propose a continuous improvement plan. Best practice is implemented when an evaluation is made of the practices of the organisation with regard to its employee assistance programme, with the aim of formulating guidelines for the strengthening of the EAP to deal effectively with preventative, as well as reactive, measures. Such guidelines for best practice are discussed with the relevant stakeholders during feedback sessions. Some of these are summarised below in Table 12.1.

Table 12.1: Survival strategies for EAPs

Theme	Sub-theme
Expanding EAP mission Broader mission, focusing more on prevention and overall employee and organisational wellbeing.	**Unchanged primary purpose.** The primary purpose for most organisations remains unchanged. **Spin-off programmes.** Some organisations create spin-off programmes that serve non-employee populations (e.g. students and refugees).
Service changes The addition of many new services beyond EAP core services.	**Continuing to offer basic services.** Core technology services such as assessment, short-term counselling and referral still offered. **Expanding services.** The addition of new services such as executive coaching, organisational development, and disability management. **Integration.** Standard services often include work-life balance, wellness, and learning and development.

Theme	Sub-theme
Specialisation Increased specialisation in internal processes as well as products and services.	**Task specialisation.** Staff dedicated exclusively to narrower focused tasks such as intake, case management, or sales. **Staff specialisation.** Hiring of professional business and sales staff. **Programme specialisation.** Creating specialised programmes for specific populations, such as physicians, lawyers, and employees in higher education.
Demonstrating value Increased need to show the value of the EAP.	**Visibility.** Increase visibility of the programme through on-site services, newsletters, and social media. **Relationships.** Foster relationships with individuals at client companies. **Utilisation of reports.** More comprehensive and aesthetically pleasing reports. **Effectiveness evaluations.** Introduce outcomes and ROI measures.
Offering more choices More customisation and access choices for clients.	**Unbundling.** Offering services such as consultation or on-site crisis services on a fee-for-service basis. **Communication modality.** More accessible methods such as instant messaging and video counselling.
Rebranding Changing EAP name and descriptors to change public perception of the company.	**Changing name.** Shortening name and removing reference to EAP to reflect broader service offerings. **Changing descriptors.** Describing services more broadly to promote ancillary offerings such as wellness and consulting.
Improving efficiency Improved efficiency in order to reduce operating costs.	**New technology.** Use of internet-based services and sophisticated databases. **Contracting out.** Using outside contractors to provide specialised services, such as crisis counselling, wellness, and work-life balance counselling.

A study conducted by Sieberhagen, Pienaar and Els[434] indicated that seven of sixteen organisations involved in measuring the effectiveness of their EAPs focused on aspects such as utilisation rates, absenteeism, reporting of chronic diseases and buy-in. Although these aspects were considered, the organisations claimed that they are not true measures of effectiveness, however. Nine of the organisations indicated that they could measure the effectiveness of their EAPs by considering utilisation rates and feedback from employees and by measuring absenteeism.

Fourteen of these organisations felt that they could improve the delivery of EAP by:[435]

- making their programmes more holistic and integrated;
- increasing the allocation of resources and personnel;
- providing their EAP in-house;
- assessing their EAP accurately;
- focusing on targeted interventions;
- improving training;
- conducting follow-ups on interventions;
- considering new ideas relevant to their EAPs;
- achieving a better return on investment;
- providing more support to employees;
- improving communication and marketing; and
- improving co-ordinator focus on wellness programmes.

A study by Courtois, Hajek, Kennish, Paul, Seward, Stockert and Thompson[436] indicated that EAPs can be assessed in a variety of ways. They considered the following to be key aspects of a programme that will influence the creation of common, measurable outcomes:

- Account management.
- Client/participant satisfaction.
- Clinical quality.
- Communication and promotional materials.
- Critical Incident Stress Management service satisfaction.
- Customer service.
- Employer/purchaser satisfaction.
- Implementation.

- Network development.
- Reporting.
- Training and education.
- Utilisation.
- Website capabilities.

They also went further to develop indicators that can be measured (see the attached annexure).

The various principles, tools and processes that can be applied for the continuous improvement of EAP initiatives in the workplace

Regardless of the size of the organisation, strategically integrated wellness programmes have six strong pillars that simultaneously support their success. If well-constructed, organisations can benefit from implementing these pillars in their wellness programmes.

According to Berry, Mirabito and Baun,[437] these pillars are as follows:

1. ***Multi-level leadership:*** creating a culture of health takes passionate, persistent and persuasive leadership at all levels of the organisation.
2. ***Alignment:*** a wellness programme should be an extension of the organisation's identity and aspirations. A cultural shift requires a great deal of effort and time.
3. ***Scope, relevance and quality:*** wellness programmes must be comprehensive, engaging and nothing less than excellent in order for employees to participate.
4. ***Accessibility:*** the aim is to make low- or no-cost services a priority. True on-site integration is essential and in this case convenience matters.
5. ***Partnerships:*** there should be an active on-going collaboration with internal and external partners that are able to provide a programme with some of its essential components and many of its desirable enhancements.
6. ***Communications:*** wellness is not just a mission, but a message. How the message is delivered can make a big difference; it should be delivered with sensitivity, creativity and media diversity.

THE ROLE OF THE EAP MANAGER IN IMPLEMENTING CONTINUOUS IMPROVEMENT

Employee assistance practitioners' continuous improvement plans could focus on programme design, implementation and networking. Govender[438] described the following as activities of EAP managers and practitioners in pursuit of continuous improvement:

Programme design: EAP design refers to a complete overview of the programme along with the targeted outcomes at which the programme is aimed.[439] EAP practitioners should conduct evaluation and research, partnering with stakeholders in measuring the impact of their EAP on the organisation and employees. Such research will provide an opportunity for stakeholders to become directly involved with the EAP in "reviewing" the programme model and in addressing areas of weakness. This participation can be formalised into an advisory committee. EAP training may be another way for EAP personnel to engage stakeholders by providing them with detailed information on EAP practice and give them an opportunity to consider their support and involvement. EAP training institutions need to increase their focus on programme design issues and equip EAP practitioners with knowledge and skills in this area.

EAP implementation: gaps identified in an EAP's implementation can be used to develop continuous improvements. Practitioners and managers could partner with EAPA-SA or its local chapters to educate their organisations on EAPs and provide support in implementing or strengthening their existing EAPs. EAP personnel need to ensure that they are involved in continuous specific professional development to build their competencies. Training institutions, EAPA-SA and EAP managers should strengthen EAP personnel competencies in the service areas of organisational consultation and EAP training, so that they can optimise the value of programmes to their organisations. Employers' perceptions regarding the importance of having healthy employees are important, because an integral part of implementing health-promoting policies and programmes in the workplace is obtaining support from those in managerial or leadership roles.[440]

EAP networking: managers need to consider building a network of support structures that are relevant to their organisations. Programmes implemented in the new millennium have the benefit of established guidelines for practice and may also bring new information into the field, especially around programming issues, yet there has been limited impact on the development of EAP standards in older, existing EAPs.

To attract and retain millennials, as well as to better serve their needs, many employers and employee assistance managers are beginning to develop innovative and content-rich EAP messages for young employees in multiple traditional and new-media formats. Strategies for ensuring that EAPs are reaching younger employees include the following:

- ***Increased use of technology:*** younger employees are generally very comfortable with (and often inseparable from) technology. Efforts to make EAP services more accessible include online, interactive assessments of drug and alcohol use, stress levels, and depression; online, interactive scenarios that teach managers to assess troubling employee situations, including when to refer to EAPs, contact human resources, call the police, or make physician referrals; webinars and podcasts on various subjects; text messaging to facilitate communication between subscribed members; and e-mails providing non-clinical support, such as coaching.
- ***New promotional materials:*** EAPs are redesigning their websites, posters, brochures, wallet cards, and other printed material to be more appealing to younger employees. They are using streamlined fonts, brighter colours, more modern designs, and more contemporary messages.
- ***New topics for seminars:*** EAPs are finding that certain topics for brown-bag lunches and other presentations tend to attract younger employees and they are updating their seminars to be more appealing to millennials. Topics on time management, financial issues, and stress are reported as popular with younger employees.
- ***Creative "take-aways":*** many EAPs participate in employer-sponsored health or benefits fairs informing employees of available services. Because some people have a natural reluctance to visit a booth associated with "personal problems", EAPs generally try to have activities or small gifts to attract people to their booth. Stress dots (small stick-on dots that measure galvanic skin response to show stress levels) are proving very popular with younger employees, as are games, squeeze toys, and other stress-reduction gifts.
- ***Work-life coordination:*** EAPs are increasingly involved in administering and promoting work-life programmes, such as telework and flexible schedules. The idea is to encourage young employees to seek assistance for a wide range of issues, including mental health and addiction problems.
- ***Mediation services:*** some EAP practitioners find that offering mediation and conflict resolution services gives them a good entrée with younger employees who may be having difficulties adjusting to the expectations of their managers or co-workers.
- ***Retention strategies:*** some EAPs are coordinating with human resource efforts to retain younger employees. The visibility of EAPs in strategic workforce planning can positively contribute to employee perceptions of EAPs as "go to" resources for advice about workplace and personal issues. For example, some employers have worked with their EAPs to design programmes for employees with zero to five years of service that offer a variety of professional and personal development activities, to create friendships and support for new employees.

CONCLUSION

Sound insight into continuous improvement initiatives is critical to assist you in ensuring a sustainable EAP in your organisation. It is imperative to use this knowledge to initiate improvement plans for your organisation's EAP.

APPENDIX

PERFORMANCE MEASURES

The following performance measures represent common metrics currently used in the EAP industry. A sub-set of the measures is listed below.

PERFORMANCE AREA

Implementation

- An implementation plan is established and customised for the client. A template is provided in which all bids and proposals to customer organisations are described. This includes steps required, timelines and the responsibilities of the EAP and customer organisation.
- Vendor has completed its implementation duties in conformance with the dates established in the mutually agreed upon implementation plan.

Network development

- Access to a provider who has two years of substance abuse or EAP experience for all counsellors and affiliates of a CEAP, or those eligible for a CEAP; 90% of employees have access to at least one EAP network provider within a distance of:
  - 10 kilometres/10 minutes for urban locations;
  - 25 kilometres/25 minutes for suburban locations; and
  - 60 kilometres/60 minutes for rural locations.
- 90% of members provide a positive response about the provider's sensitivity to cultural and ethnic backgrounds.
- 90% of members provide a positive response regarding their overall satisfaction with the affiliate's availability.
- 90% of members provide a positive response regarding the accessibility of affiliates.
- Providers must have a Masters level degree, an independent licence to practice and be CEAP-eligible, with three years of EAP experience.

Customer and member services

- Routine EAP appointments are scheduled within three business days unless requested otherwise by a participant.

- 100% of urgent callers will be offered an assessment session(s) within one business day of contacting the EAP.
- 100% of emergency calls have same-day access to care and their disposition is followed up closely. If a referral is necessary, 95% of all referrals for in-person sessions will be referred to a counsellor on the same day, or within 24 hours.

Member satisfaction

- 100% of members attending workplace training will be given an evaluation form soliciting their feedback.

REFERENCES

Acts Online. 2013. *Promotion of Access to Information Act, 2000 (Act No. 2 of 2000)*. Retrieved from https://www.acts.co.za/promotion-of-access-to-information-act-2000/index.html on 08.08.2016.

Adigun, AO, & Bello, BA. 2012. Influence of employee assistance programmes on commitment in manufacturing companies in Lagos state. *International Journal of Information Technology and Business Management, 26*(1): 38-43.

American Psychiatric Association. 2013. *Diagnostic and statistical manual of mental disorders: DSM-5*. Arlington, VA: American Psychiatric Association.

Andrews, CM, Shin, HC, Marsh, JC, & Cao, D. 2013. Client and program characteristics associated with wait time to substance abuse treatment entry. *The American Journal of Drug and Alcohol Abuse, 39*(1): 61-68.

Center for Mental Health Services. 2008. *An employee's guide to employee assistance programs*. Retrieved from https://www.businessgrouphealth.org/pub/?id=f31372a2-2354-d714-51e4-ae4127ced552 on 20.11.2017.

Annandale, M. 2012. *An empirical investigation into the impact of work-life balance practices on employees and employers*. Stellenbosch: Stellenbosch University. (Doctoral dissertation.)

Beidel, B, & Brennan, K. 2005. Health and wellness and productivity: best practice requires EAP involvement. *EAPA International*: 35-36.

Bell, NJ. 2003. *A needs assessment for an employee assistance programme (EAP) for the Department of Water Affairs and Forestry in the Northern Province*. Pretoria: University of South Africa. (Unpublished Master's dissertation.)

Berridge, JR, & Cooper, CL. 1993. Stress and coping in US organizations: the role of the employee assistance programme. *Work & Stress, 7*(1): 89-102.

Berridge, JR, & Cooper, CL. 1994. The employee assistance programme: its role in organizational coping and excellence. *Personnel Review, 23*(7): 4-20.

Berry, LL, Mirabito, AM, & Baun, WB. 2010. What's the hard return on employee wellness programs? *Harvard Business Review, 88*(12): 104-112.

Bhagat, RS, Steverson, PK, & Segovis, JC. 2007. International and cultural variations in employee assistance programmes: implications for managerial health and effectiveness. *Journal of Management Studies, 44*(2): 222-242.

Bophela, N, & Govender, P. 2015. Employee assistance programs (EAPs): tools for quality of work life. *Problems and Perspectives in Management*, 13(2): 506-514.

Boyce, LA, Jeffrey Jackson, R, & Neal, LJ. 2010. Building successful leadership coaching relationships: examining impact of matching criteria in a leadership coaching program. *Journal of Management Development, 29*(10): 914-931.

Brecher, B. 2014. What is professional ethics? *Nursing Ethics, 21*(2): 239-244.

Brink, A. 2002. *Die aanwending van werknemers-hulpprogramme deur welsynsinstansies*. Pretoria: University of South Africa. (Unpublished Master's dissertation.)

Carroll, AB. 1989. *Business and society: ethics and stakeholder management*. Cincinnati, OH: South-Western.

Chase, YE. 2015. Professional ethics: complex issues for the social work profession. *Journal of Human Behavior in the Social Environment*, 25(7): 766-773.

Courtois, PH, Hajek, M, Kennish, R, Paul, R, Seward, K, Stockert, TJ, & Thompson, C. 2005. Performance measures in the employee assistance program. *Employee Assistance Quarterly, 19*(3): 45-58. DOI: 10.1300/J022v19n03_0.

Csiernik, R. 1995. A review of research methods used to examine employee assistance delivery options. *Evaluation and Program Planning*, 18(1): 25-36.

Csiernik, R. 1998. An integrated model of occupational assistance. *The Social Worker, 66*(3): 37-47.

Csiernik, R. 2005. What we're doing in EAP: meeting the challenge of an integrated model of practice. *Journal of Employee Assistance and Workplace Behavioral Health, 21*(1): 11-22.

Csiernik, R & Csiernik, A. 2012. Canadian employee assistance programming: an overview. *Journal of Workplace Behavioral Health, 27*(2): 100-116

Daniels, S. 1997. Employee assistance programmes. *Work Study, 46*(7): 251-253.

Da Veiga, A. 2017. Ethical and privacy considerations for research. In: Martins, N, Martins, EC, & Viljoen, R. *Organisational diagnosis: tools and applications for practitioners and researchers.* Randburg: KR Publishing: 273-311.

Dawad, S, & Hoque, M. 2016. Employees' awareness, attitudes and utilisation of an employee wellness programme in a financial services company in South Africa. *Occupational Health Southern Africa, 22(6),* 19-22.

Department of Public Service and Administration – Republic of South Africa. 2011. *Employee health and wellness strategic framework for the public service.* Retrieved from www.dpsa.gov.za/about.php?id=6;download on 14.02.2012.

Dessler, G. 1997. *Human resource management.* 7th edition. Upper Saddle River, NJ: Prentice-Hall.

American Psychiatric Association. 2013. *Diagnostic and statistical manual of mental disorders: DSM-5.* Arlington, VA: American Psychiatric Association.

Dickman, F. 1985. Employee assistance programs: history and philosophy. In: Dickman, F, Emerner, WG, Hutchison, WS (eds.). *Counselling the troubled person in industry: a guide to the organization, implementation, and evaluation of employee assistance programs.* Springfield, IL: Charles C. Thomas Publishers: 7-12.

Donaldson, SJ, & Ko, IA. 2010. Positive organizational psychology, behaviour, and scholarship: a review of the emerging literature and evidence base. *The Journal of Positive Psychology, 5*(3): 177-191.

Dormody, TJ, & Seevers, BS. 1994. Predicting youth leadership life skills development among FFA members in Arizona, Colorado, and New Mexico. *Journal of Agricultural Education, 35*(2): 65-71.

Dreyfus, EA. 2005. *Coaching and psychotherapy.* Retrieved from https://www.planetpsych.com on 14.02.2012.

DuBrin, AJ. 2004. *Applying psychology. Individual and organizational effectiveness.* 6th edition. Upper Saddle River, NJ: Prentice Hall. Pearson.

Du Plessis, A. 1991. A society in transition: EAP in South Africa. *EAP Digest, 11*(3): 35-66.

Du Plessis, A. 1998. Employee Assistance Programmes. *Social Work Practice, 1*(1): 23-25.

EAPA-SA. 2010. *The Code of Ethics.* Retrieved from http://www.eapasa.co.za on 09.08.2016.

EAP Workgroup. 2007. *EASNA website.* Retrieved from http://www.easna.org. on 30.08.2017.

EAP Workgroup Subcommittee. 2007. *EASNA website.* Retrieved from http://www.easna.org on 30.08.2017.

Employee Assistance Professionals Association of South Africa (EAPA-SA). 1999. *Standards for employee assistance programmes: from micro to macro practice. EAP in practice in the South African context.* Hatfield: Standards Committee of EAPA-SA.

Employee Assistance Professionals Association of South Africa (EAPA-SA). 2005. *Standards for employee assistance programs in South Africa.* Hatfield: Standards Committee of EAPA-SA.

Employee Assistance Professionals Association. (2010). *EAPA Standards and Professional Guidelines for Employee Assistance Programs.* Arlington, VA: Author. Retrieved from http://www.eapassn.org on 30.08.2017.

Esterhuizen, W. 2015. *Organisational culture of shift workers in the healthcare environment.* Pretoria: University of South Africa. (Unpublished Doctoral thesis.)

Ford, DJ, & Pasmore, WA. 2006. Vision: friend or foe during change. *Journal of Applied Behavioral Change, 42*(2): 172-176.

Gerber, M. 1995. Employee assistance: combining communication and organizational development. *Human Resources Management*, 11(4): 31-34

Gladstone, J, & Reynolds, T. 1997. Single session group work intervention in response to employee stress during workforce transformation. *Social Work with Groups*, *20*(1): 33-49.

Govender, T. 2009. *A critical analysis of the prevalence and nature of employee assistance programmes in the Eastern Cape Buffalo City municipal area.* Pretoria: University of Pretoria. (Unpublished MSD EAP thesis.)

Govender, T. 2011. Dynamic EA and wellness needed: wellness-EAP. *HR Future*, 48.

Grant, AM. 2003. The impact of life coaching on goal attainment, metacognition and mental health. *Social Behavior and Personality*, *31*(3): 253-264.

Grobler, A & Joubert, YT. 2012. Expectations, perceptions and experience of EAP services in the SAPS. *Journal of Contemporary Management*, *9*: 150-171.

Grobler, A & Maree, C. 2009. *The value and extent of religious participation of the South African Police Service's employees; Expectations, perceptions and experience of the South African Police Service's employees regarding the Employee Assistance Services (EAS).* (Unpublished report.)

Hamdulay, A. 2014a. A virtuous circle of health: stress management-wellness. *HR Future*: 37.

Hamdulay, A. 2014b. Manage mental illness in the workplace: wellness-proactive management. *HR Future*: 28.

Highley, JC, & Cooper, CL. 1994. Evaluating EAPs. *Personnel Review*, *23*(7): 46-59.

HPCSA (Health Professions Council of South Africa). 2012. *Professional board for psychology rules of conduct pertaining specifically to psychology.* Retrieved from www.hpcsa.co.za/board_psychology.php on 17.05.2016.

International Employee Assistance Professionals Association. 2009. *About employee assistance.* Retrieved from http://www.eapassn.org/i4a/pages/index.cfm?pageid=869 on 10.10.2017.

Jacobson, JM, & Attridge, M. 2010. Employee assistance programs (EAPs): an allied profession for work/life. In Sweet, S, & Casey, J (eds.). *Sloan work and family research network.* Retrieved from https://wfnetwork.bc.edu/encyclopedia_entry on 06.03.2016.

Jacobson, MJ. 2012. Risk of compassion fatigue and burnout and potential for compassion satisfaction among employee assistance professionals: protecting the workforce. *Traumatology 18*(3): 64-72.

Janićijević, N. 2010. Business processes in organizational diagnosis. *Management*, *15*(2): 85-106.

Jantjie, KTG. 2009. *Challenges of HIV and aids experienced by working women: the role and response of employee assistance programme.* Pretoria: University of Pretoria. (Unpublished MSD EAP thesis.)

Joseph, B, & Walker, A. 2017. Employee assistance programs in Australia: the perspectives of organisational leaders across sectors. *Asia Pacific Journal of Human Resources*, 55(2): 177-191.

Kanter, RM. 1977. *Work and family in the United States: a critical review and agenda for research and policy.* New York: Russell Sage Foundation.

Kessler, RC, Berguland, P, Demler, O, Jin, R,Koretz, D, Merikangas, KR, Rush, AJ, Walters, EE & Wang, PS. 2003. The epidemiology of major depressive disorder: results from the National Comorbidity Survey Replication (NCS-R). *Journal of American Medical Association*, 283(23): 3095-3105.

Kessler, RC, Ames, M, Hymel, PA, Loeppke, R, McKenas, DK, Tichling, DE, Stung, PE & Ustun, TB. 2004. Using the World Health Organization Health and Work Performance Questionnaire (HPQ) to evaluate the indirect workplace costs of illness. *Journal of Occupational and Environmental Medicine*, *46*: 523-537.

Kim, S, Egan, TM, Kim, W, & Kim, J. 2013. The impact of managerial coaching behavior on employee work-related reactions. *Journal of Business and Psychology*, *28*(3): 315-330.

Knapp, S, Handelsman, MM, Gottlieb, MC, & Vandecreek, LD. 2013. The dark side of professional ethics professional psychology. *Research and Practice*, *44*(6): 371-377.

Kossek, E, Kaliath, T, & Kaliath, P. 2012 Achieving employee wellbeing in a changing work environment An expert commentary on current scholarship. *International Journal of Manpower, 33*(7):738-753.

Kumar, A, & Parashar, D. 2012. Challenges and opportunities in HIV/AIDS counselling: a case of Jharkhand. *Journal of Human Behavior in the Social Environment, 22*(2): 148-152.

Kunte, M. 2016. Employee wellness practices – a study in selected organizations. *International Journal of Innovative Research and Advanced Studies, 3*(12): 334-337.

Kurzman, PA. 2013. Employee assistance programs for the new millennium: emergence of the comprehensive model. *Social Work in Mental Health, 11*(5): 381-403.

Ledimo, O. 2017. Preparing and involving all stakeholders. In: Martins, N, Martins, EC, & Viljoen, R. *Organisational diagnosis: tools and applications for practitioners and researchers.* Chapter 2. Randburg: KR Publishing: 25-38.

Lee, CH, & Bruvold, NT. 2003. Creating value for employees: investment in employee development. *The International Journal of Human Resource Management, 14*(6): 981-1000.

Lewis, JA, & Lewis, MO. 1986. *Counselling programs for employees in the workplace.* California: Brooks/Cole.

Martins, EC, & Ledimo, O. 2017a. Developing and sourcing assessment instruments. In: Martins, N, Martins, EC, & Viljoen, R. *Organisational diagnosis: tools and applications for practitioners and researchers.* Chapter 4. KR Publishing: Randburg: 85-112.

Martins, EC, & Ledimo, O. 2017b. Survey administration process. In: Martins, N, Martins, EC, & Viljoen, R. *Organisational diagnosis: tools and applications for practitioners and researchers.* Chapter 3. KR Publishing: Randburg: 39-84.

Masi, DA. 2011. Redefining the EAP field. *Journal of Workplace Behavioral Health, 26*(1): 1-9.

Mathlape, MG. 2003. Strategic positioning of EAP in South African workplaces. *Acta Commercii, 3*(1): 29-38.

Mchunu, G. (2012). Proposed guidelines for a workplace health promotion policy and implementation framework. *Occupational Health Southern Africa, 18*(2): 5- 12.

McMahon, G, & Palmer, S. 2014. *Handbook of counselling.* New York: Routledge.

Milner, KMA, Greylin, M, Goetzel, RZ, Da Silva, R, Kolber-Alexander, T, Patel, DMD, Tabrizi, MJMS, Nosel, C & Beckowiski, MMPH (2013). The Healthiest Company Index: A Campaign to Promote Worksite Wellness in South Africa. *Journal of Occupational and Environmental Medicine, 55*(2): 172–178.

Milot, M. 2017. Evaluating benefit equity in outcomes among users of an employee assistance program. *EASNA Research Notes, 6*(3): 1-7.

Mines, RA, Anderson, S, & Von Stroh, P. 1991. EAP ethics and the professions: the application of ethical principles is perhaps more vital to EAPs that serve the professions than to any other client base. *EAPA Exchange,* December: 26-29.

Mogorosi, LD. 1997. *Employee assistance at the workplace: the South African experiences and model.* New York: Columbia University. (Unpublished Doctoral dissertation.)

Mogorosi, L. 2009. Employee assistance programmes: their rationale, basic principles and essential elements. *Social Work/Maatskaplike Werk, 45*(4): 343-359.

Murphy, LR. 1995. Managing job stress: an employee assistance/human resource management partnership. *Personnel Review, 24*(1): 41-50.

Muto, T, Fujimori, Y, & Suzuki, K. 2004. Characteristics of an external employee assistance programme in Japan. *Occupational Medicine, 54*(8): 570-575.

Nagesar, N. 2013. *The development of an employee assistance programme (EAP) model for secondary school educators in Kwazulu-Natal: an exploratory study.* Durban: Durban University of Technology. (Unpublished thesis.)

Nair, P. & Xavier, M. 2012. Initiating an employee assistance program (EAP) for a corporate: an experiential learning. *The IUP Journal of Organizational Behavior, XI*(2): 67-75.

Nakao, M, Nishikitani, M, Shima, S, & Yano, E. 2007. A 2-year cohort study on the impact of an employee assistance programme (EAP) on depression and suicidal thoughts in male Japanese workers. *International Archives of Occupational and Environmental Health, 81*(2): 151-157.

Ndhlovu, MJ. 2010. *Exploring positive psychological strengths in employees attending EAP in the public service: a qualitative study.* Pretoria: University of South Africa. (Unpublished Doctoral thesis.)

Nyati, F. 2012. Encourage employee wellness: wellness-more to life. *HR Future*: 47.

Nyati, F. 2013. Set up integrated health and wellness programmes: more to life-wellness. *HR Future*: 48-49.

Padachy, I. 1996. *An employee assistance programme as applies in a white-collar environment.* Pretoria: University of South Africa. (Unpublished dissertation.)

Panhwar, IA, Channar, ZA, Pasha, MA, & Memon, FN. 2015. Impact of employee assistance program on employee satisfaction of public and private organizations of Sindh. *Grassroots, 49*(1).

Pescud, M, Teal, R, Shilton, T, Slevin, T, Ledger, M, Waterworth, P, & Rosenberg, M. 2015. Employers' views on the promotion of workplace health and wellbeing: a qualitative study. *BMC Public Health, 15*: 2-10.

Prinsloo, R. 2015. Group intervention with institutionalised older persons. *HTS Theological Studies, 71*(3): 1-7.

Public Service Commission (PSC). 2006. *Evaluation of employee assistance programmes in the public service.* Pretoria. Public Service Commission.

Rajin, J. 2012. *Employee assistance programme in the South African Police Service: a case study of Moroka police station.* Pretoria: University of South Africa. (Unpublished dissertation.)

Rakepa, TT. 2012. *Assistance programme of the Department of Education: a case study of Motheo district in the Free State province.* Stellenbosch: University of Stellenbosch. (Unpublished dissertation.)

Ramokolo, ME. 2004. *The exploration of the resistance of troubled employees to utilise the employee assistance programme at Aventis Pharma.* Pretoria: University of Pretoria. (Unpublished MSD EAP thesis.)

Roberts, P. 2015. Getting more from your EAP. *Occupational Health, 67*(7): 24.

Saeed, B. and Wang, W. 2014. Sustainability Embedded Organizational Diagnostic Model. *Modern Economy*, 5, 424-431. doi: 10.4236/me.2014.54041. Retrieved from http://www.scirp.org/journal/PaperInformation.aspx?PaperID=44997 on 20.11.2016.

Sagunthala, C, & Karthikeyan, R. 2016. A study on occupational stress level of employees in textile shops with special reference to Coimbatore district. *International Journal, 4*(2): 67 -73.

Sandys, J. 2015. The evolution of employee assistance programs in the United States: a 20-year retrospective from 26 EAP vendors. *EASNA Research Notes, 5*(1): 1-16.

Schwandt, TA. 2015. Reconstructing professional ethics and responsibility: implications of critical systems thinking. *Evaluation, 21*(4): 462-466.

September, AL. 2010. *An exploratory study on the need for an employee assistance programme (EAP): the case of Cape Winelands District Municipality.* Stellenbosch: University of Stellenbosch. (Doctoral dissertation.)

Sfestani, RS, & Peykani, MH. 2017. Providing a professional ethics model for improving public accountability in the Iranian governmental organizations. *International Review of Management and Marketing, 7*(2): 415-420.

Sharf, RS. 2012. *Theories of psychotherapy and counselling: concepts and cases.* Boston: Cengage Learning, Brookes/Cole.

Sieberhagen, C, Pienaar, J, & Els, C. 2011. Management of employee wellness in South Africa: employer, service provider and union perspectives. *SA Journal of Human Resource Management, 9*(1), 1-14. doi: 10.4102/sajhrm.v9i1.305.

Slabbert, Y. 2015. Towards a new stakeholder-inclusive conceptual framework to strengthen internal corporate image. *Communicare, 34*(2), 39-57.

Sonnenstuhl, WJ, & Trice, HM. 1990. *Strategies for employee assistance programmes: the crucial balance.* 2nd edition. Cornell University: ILR Press.

South African Council for Social Service Professions. 2012. *Professional Conduct & Ethics.* Retrieved from https://www.sacssp.co.za on 06.05.2016.

Standards Committee of EAP–SA. 2010. *Standards for employee assistance programmes in South Africa.* Pretoria: EAPA South Africa Branch.

Straussner, SLA. 1989. Occupational social work today: an overview. *Employee Assistance Quarterly*, 5(1): 1-17. DOI: 10.1300/J022v05n01_01 : https://doi.org/10.1300/J022v05n01_01

Swanepoel, V. 2004. *'n Ondersoek na die behoefte aan 'n werknemerhulpprogram by die Kaapse Plan: 'n maatskaplike werk perspektief.* Pretoria: University of South Africa. (Unpublished Doctoral thesis.)

Taylor, PA, Holosko, MJ, Wayne-Smith, B, & Feit, MD. 1988. Paving the way for EAP evaluation: implications for social work. *Employee Assistance Quarterly, 3*(3/4): 69-77.

Terblanche, L. 2011. Employee assistance programmes explained: wellness-EAP. *HR Future*: 27.

Terblanche, LS. 1992. The state of the art of EAPs in South Africa: a critical analysis. *Employee Assistance Quarterly, 7*(3): 17-28.

Triner, J, & Turner, S. 2005. Professional coaches and employee assistance practitioners. *Journal of Workplace Behavioral Health, 21*(2): 1-14.

Viljoen, RC. 2015, *Organisational change and development: an African perspective.* Randburg: Knowledge Resources.

Walker, A & Joseph, B. (2017). Employee assistance programs in Australia: the perspectives of organisational leaders across sectors. *Asia Pacific Journal of Human Resources, 55*, 177–191.

Workforce Performance Solutions. *EAP client satisfaction survey.* Retrieved from https://wwwaffiliatedeap.com on 07.08.2016.

ENDNOTES

1. EAPA-SA, 2005:7.
2. Jacobson, 2012:64.
3. Rajin, 2012.
4. Taylor, Holosko, Wayne-Smith & Feit, 1988.
5. Du Plessis, 1991:20.
6. Sonnenstuhl & Trice, 1990:l.
7. Berridge, 1996:59.
8. Alker & McHugh, 2000:303.
9. Robbins & DeCenzo, 2005:248.
10. The Employee Assistance Professional Association - South Africa (EAPA-SA), 2005:5.
11. Rajin, 2012:13.
12. The International Employee Assistance Professionals Association (IEAPA), 2009.
13. Murphy, 1995.
14. Bophela, 2015.
15. Murphy, 1995.
16. Daniels, 1997.
17. Muto, Fujimori, & Suzuki, 2004.
18. Berridge & Cooper, 1993.
19. Bhagat, Steverson & Segovis, 2007.
20. Nakao, Nishikitani, Shima & Yano, 2007.
21. Csiernik & Csiernik, 2012.
22. Daniels, 1997.
23. Panhwar, Channar, Pasha & Memon, 2015.
24. Bophela, 2015.
25. Bhagat, Steverson & Segovis, 2007.
26. Joseph & Walker, 2017:190.
27. Daniels, 1997.
28. Panhwar, Channar, Pasha & Memon, 2015.
29. Csiernik & Csiernik, 2012.
30. Terblanche, 2011.
31. Gerber, 1995.
32. Bell, 2003.
33. Ndhlovu, 2010.
34. Bophela, 2015.
35. Kotze, 1997.
36. Kotze, 1997.
37. Jacobson, 2012.
38. Bergh & Theron, 2009:20.
39. Bergh & Theron, 2009.
40. Kurzman, 1992.
41. Mogorosi, 2009:344.
42. Murphy, 1995.
43. Andrew, Shin, Marsh & Cao, 2013; Bophela, 2015.
44. Bhagat, Steverson & Segovis, 2007.
45. Kumar & Parashar, 2012.
46. Gilbert, 2013.
47. Bophela, 2015.
48. Bophela, 2015.
49. Bophela, 2015.
50. Grobler & Joubert, 2012.
51. Harper, 1999.
52. Csiernik & Csiernik, 2012:115.
53. Govender, 2011.
54. Jacobson, 2012.
55. Joseph & Walker, 2017.
56. Nyati, 2013.
57. Panhwar, Channar, Pasha & Memon, 2015.
58. Terblanche, 2011.
59. Darey, McCarthy, Hill & Grady, 2012.
60. Csiernik & Csiernik, 2012.
61. Jacobson, 2012.
62. Csiernik & Csiernik, 2012.
63. Berridge & Cooper, 1993.
64. Berridge & Cooper, 1993.
65. Nyati, 2013.
66. Hamdulay, 2014.
67. Mogorosi, 2009.
68. Joseph & Walker, 2017.
69. Grobler & Joubert, 2012.
70. Kaufman & Guerra-Lopez, 2013.
71. Janićijević, 2010.
72. Joseph & Walker, 2017.
73. Govender, 2009:52.
74. Grobler & Joubert, 2012.
75. Joseph & Walker, 2017.
76. Saeed & Wang, 2014.
77. Pescud et al., 2015.
78. Joseph & Walker, 2017.
79. Nair & Xavier, 2012.
80. Daniels, 1997.
81. Mogorosi, 2009.
82. Mogorosi, 2009.
83. Leedy, 2009.
84. Gill, Stewart, Treasure & Chadwick, 2008.

85. Gill et al., 2008:291.
86. Gill et al., 2008.
87. Lambert & Loiselle, 2008.
88. Lambert & Loiselle, 2008.
89. Viljoen, 2015.
90. Wellman, Kruger & Mitchell, 2009.
91. Martins & Ledimo, 2017.
92. Leedy, 2009.
93. Martins & Ledimo, 2017.
94. Ledimo, 2017.
95. Wellmann et al., 2009.
96. Leedy, 2009.
97. Berridge & Cooper, 1993.
98. Hanisch, Birner, Oberhauser, Nowak & Sabariego, 2017.
99. Rakepa, 2012.
100. Csiernik & Csiernik, 2012.
101. Nair & Xavier, 2012.
102. Rakepa, 2012.
103. Jacobson, 2012.
104. Nair & Xavier, 2016.
105. Rakepa, 2012.
106. Hanisch et al., 2017.
107. Hawad & Hoque, 2016.
108. Nair & Xavier, 2012.
109. Joseph & Walker, 2017.
110. Govender, 2009:27.
111. Hawad & Hoque, 2016.
112. Kunte, 2016.
113. Rakepa, 2012.
114. Govender, 2009:29.
115. Joseph & Walker, 2017.
116. Dawad & Hoque, 2016.
117. Dawad & Hoque, 2016.
118. Joseph & Walker, 2017.
119. Rakepa, 2012.
120. Jacobson, 2012:64.
121. Hanisch et al., 2017.
122. Kunte, 2016.
123. Nair & Xavier, 2012.
124. Rakepa, 2012.
125. Grobler & Joubert, 2012.
126. Dawad & Hoque, 2016.
127. Mogorosi, 2009:346–348.
128. Masi, 2011.
129. Terblanche, 2011.
130. Terblanche, 2011.
131. Nair & Xavier, 2012.
132. Mogorosi, 2009:347.
133. Pescud et al., 2015.
134. Gilpsie et al., 2016.
135. American Psychiatric Association, 2013.
136. Rajin, 2012.
137. Rajin, 2012.
138. Public Service Commission, 2006:16.
139. Pescud et al., 2015.
140. Grobler & Joubert, 2012.
141. Pescud et al., 2015.
142. Pescud et al., 2015.
143. Pescud et al., 2015.
144. Kunte, 2016.
145. Rajin, 2012.
146. Berridge & Cooper, 1993; Terblanche, 2011.
147. Joseph & Walker, 2017.
148. Rajin, 2012.
149. Rakepa, 2012.
150. EAPA-SA, 1999:8–15.
151. Terblanche, 2011.
152. Berridge & Cooper, 1993.
153. Rajin, 2012; Rakepa, 2012.
154. Rakepa, 2012:31.
155. EAP-SA, 1999:20.
156. Berridge & Cooper, 1993.
157. Joseph & Walker, 2017.
158. Joseph & Walker, 2017.
159. Rajin, 2012.
160. Terblanche, 2011.
161. Rakepa, 2012:32.
162. Straussner, 1990.
163. Dessler, 1997:524.
164. Rajin, 2012.
165. Sharar, 2008.
166. Rajin, 2012.
167. Pescud et al., 2015.
168. Berridge & Cooper, 1994.
169. Govender, 2009.
170. Grobler & Joubert, 2012.
171. Grobler & Joubert, 2012.
172. Rajin, 2012.
173. Govender, 2009; Rajin, 2012; Pescud et al., 2015.
174. Govender, 2009; Rajin, 2012; Pescud et al., 2015.
175. Govender, 2009; Rajin, 2012; Pescud et al., 2015.

176. Hanisch et al., 2016.
177. Govender, 2009.
178. Mogorosi, 2009:45.
179. Rajin, 2012.
180. Pescud et al., 2015.
181. Hanisch et al., 2017.
182. Berridge & Cooper, 1994.
183. Govender, 2009.
184. Joseph & Walker, 2016.
185. Mogorosi, 2009.
186. Pescud et al., 2015.
187. Mogorosi, 2009.
188. Rajin, 2012.
189. Hoque, 2016.
190. Joseph & Walker, 2016.
191. Milot, 2017.
192. Milot, 2017.
193. Nair & Xavier, 2012.
194. Sharf, 2012.
195. McMahon & Palmer, 2014.
196. Sagunthala & Karthikeyan, 2016.
197. Rajin, 2012.
198. Nair & Xavier, 2012.
199. Rajin, 2012:24.
200. Dawad & Hoque, 2016.
201. Govender, 2009.
202. Rakepa, 2012.
203. Sharf, 2012:6–7.
204. Nagesar, 2013.
205. Govender, 2009:65.
206. Dreyfus, 2005; Grant, 2003.
207. Sharf, 2012.
208. Kim, Egan, Kim & Kim, 2013.
209. Nagesar, 2013.
210. Boyce, Jackson & Neal, 2010.
211. Nagesar, 2013:75.
212. Dreyfus, 2005; Grant, 2003.
213. Govender, 2009:60.
214. Prinsloo, 2015.
215. Gladstone & Reynolds, 1997.
216. EAPA, 2003:49.
217. Nagesar, 2013.
218. Sharf, 2012.
219. Sharf, 2012; Nagesar, 2013.
220. Sagunthala & Karthikeyan, 2016.
221. Dormody & Seevers, 1995.
222. Lee & Bruvild, 2003.
223. Bell, 2003.
224. Swanepoel, 2004.
225. Nagesar, 2013.
226. Govender, 2009.
227. Rakepa, 2012.
228. Nagesar, 2013.
229. Govender, 2009.
230. Kunte, 2016.
231. Rakepa, 2012.
232. Kunte, 2016.
233. Seligman & Csikszentmihalyi, 2000.
234. Nagesar, 2013.
235. Pescud et al., 2015.
236. Rakepa, 2012.
237. Pescud et al., 2015.
238. Kunte, 2016.
239. Nagesar, 2013:78.
240. Rakepa, 2012:21.
241. Pescud et al., 2015.
242. Kunte, 2016.
243. Rakepa, 2012.
244. Nagesar, 2013.
245. Pescud et al. 2015.
246. Esterhuizen, 2014.
247. Matlhape, 2003.
248. Benn, Abratt & O'Leary, 2016.
249. Ledimo, 2017.
250. Caroll, 1989.
251. Mogorosi, 2009.
252. Ledimo, 2017.
253. Slabbert, 2015.
254. Ledimo, 2017.
255. Ledimo, 2017.
256. Ledimo, 2017.
257. Ledimo, 2017.
258. Csiernik & Csiernik, 2012.
259. Mogorosi, 2009.
260. Rakepa, 2012:32.
261. Rakepa, 2012.
262. Mogorosi, 2009.
263. Milner et al., 2013.
264. Rakepa, 2012.
265. Mogorosi, 2009.
266. Milner et al., 2013.
267. Du Plessis, 1988:24.
268. Mogorosi, 2009.
269. Mogorosi, 2009.

270. Rajin, 2012.
271. Govender, 2009.
272. Ramokolo, 2004.
273. Rakepa, 2012.
274. Govender, 2009.
275. Csiernik & Csiernik, 2012.
276. Terblanche, 1992.
277. Rakepa, 2012.
278. Mogorosi, 2009.
279. Rajin, 2012.
280. Mogorosi, 2009.
281. Nagesar, 2013.
282. Mogorosi, 2009.
283. Roberts, 2015.
284. Nagesar, 2013.
285. Govender, 2009.
286. Nagesar, 2013.
287. Chase, 2015:766.
288. Knapp, Handelsman, Gottlieb & Vandecreek, 2013.
289. Brecher, 2014.
290. Govender, 2009.
291. Govender, 2009.
292. Brecher, 2014.
293. Sharf, 2012.
294. EAP, 2009.
295. Mogorosi, 2009.
296. Grobler & Joubert, 2012:152.
297. Govender, 2009.
298. Chase, 2015.
299. Mogorosi, 2009.
300. De Veiga, 2017:280.
301. Chase, 2015.
302. Rajin, 2012.
303. De Veiga, 2017.
304. Rajin, 2012.
305. Rakepa, 2012.
306. Rakepa, 2012.
307. Sharf, 2012.
308. Chase, 2015:765.
309. Mines, Anderson & Von Stroh, 1991.
310. Govender, 2009.
311. Chase, 2015.
312. Mines et al., 1991.
313. Nagesar, 2013.
314. Knapp et al., 2013.
315. Chase, 2015.
316. Chase, 2015.
317. Schwandt, 2015:464.
318. Brecher, 2014.
319. Mines et al., 1991:27.
320. Schwandt, 2015.
321. Knapp et al., 2013.
322. Knapp et al., 2013.
323. Brecher, 2014:243.
324. Schwandt, 2015.
325. Brecher, 2014.
326. Knapp et al., 2013.
327. Chase, 2015.
328. Brecher, 2014.
329. Knapp, 2013.
330. Sfestani & Peykani, 2017.
331. Chase, 2015.
332. Sfestani & Peykani, 2017.
333. Knapp et al., 2013:371.
334. Peykani, 2017.
335. Chase, 2015.
336. Brecher, 2014.
337. Lewis & Lewis, 1986.
338. DuBrin, 2004.
339. Govender, 2009.
340. Grobler & Joubert, 2012.
341. Govender, 2009.
342. EAPA-SA, 1999.
343. Ford & Pasmore, 2006.
344. EAP Workgroup, 2007.
345. EAP Workgroup Subcommittee, 2007.
346. Grobler & Joubert, 2012.
347. DPSA, 2011:1, cited in Grobler & Joubert, 2012.
348. South African Council for Social Service Professions, 2012:1; HPCSA, 2012:1.
349. Grobler & Maree, 2009:28.
350. Grobler & Maree, 2009:28.
351. Grobler & Joubert, 2012.
352. Jacobson, 2012.
353. Annandale, 2012.
354. Kanter, 1977.
355. Jacobson & Attridge, 2010.
356. Mchunu, 2012.
357. DuBrin, 2004.
358. DuBrin, 2004.
359. Donaldson & Ko, 2010.
360. Mogorosi, 2009.

361. Rakepa, 2012.
362. Jantjie, 2009.
363. DuBrin, 2004.
364. Milner, Greylin, Goetzel, Da Silva, Kolber-Alexander, Patel, Nosel & Beckowiski, 2013.
365. Milner et al., 2013.
366. Peters, 2008.
367. Grobler & Joubert, 2012.
368. Grobler & Joubert, 2012.
369. Padachy, 1996.
370. Brink, 2002.
371. Brink, 2002.
372. Mogorosi, 2009
373. Kossek, Kaliath & Kaliath, 2012.
374. EAPA-SA, 1999.
375. Beidel & Brennan, 2005:36.
376. Csiernik, 1998.
377 Sharf, 2012.
378. Da Veiga, 2017.
379. PoPI, 2013.
380. Da Veiga, 2017; PoPI, 2013:14.
381. Sharf, 2012.
382. Sharf, 2012.
383. Da Veiga, 2017.
384. EAPA-SA, 2005:7.
385. Govender, 2009.
386. Govender, 2009:51.
387. Govender, 2009.
388. Govender, 2009.
389. Dickman, 1985.
390. Govender, 2009.
391. EAPA-SA, 2005:6.
392. Rajin, 2012.
393. Govender, 2009.
394. EAPA-SA, 2005:24.
395. Govender, 2009.
396. Mogorosi, 2009.
397. Govender, 2009.
398. EAPA-SA, 2005:14.
399. Highly & Cooper, 1994.
400. Govender, 2009.
401. Milot, 2017.
402. Milot, 2017.
403. Milot, 2017.
404. Mogorosi, 2009.
405. Govender, 2009.
406. Walker & Joseph, 2017.
407. Mogorosi, 2009.
408. Walker & Joseph, 2017.
409. Walker & Joseph, 2017.
410. Mogorosi, 2009.
411. Mogorosi, 2009.
412. Mogorosi, 2009.
413. Govender, 2009.
414. Mogorosi, 2009:352.
415. Mogorosi, 2009.
416. Highly & Cooper, 1994.
417. Milot, 2017.
418. Mogorosi, 2009.
419. Walker & Joseph, 2017.
420. Sieberhagen, Pienaar & Els, 2011.
421. Hoque, 2016.
422. Walker & Joseph, 2017.
423. Kunte, 2016.
424. Walker & Joseph, 2017.
425. Walker & Joseph, 2017.
426. Govender, 2009.
427. Rakepa, 2012.
428. Martins & Ledimo, 2017.
429. Rakepa, 2012.
430. Kessler et al., 2003; 2004.
431. Jacobson & Attridge, 2010.
432. Martins & Ledimo, 2017.
433. Walker & Joseph, 2017.
434. Sieberhagen, Pienaar & Els, 2011.
435. Sieberhagen, Pienaar & Els, 2011.
436. Courtois, Hajek, Kennish, Paul, Seward, Stockert & Thompson, 2004.
437. Berry, Mirabito & Baun, 2010.
438. Govender, 2009.
439. Kunte, 2016.
440. Pescud et al., 2015.

Index

C

D

www.ingramcontent.com/pod-product-compliance
Lightning Source LLC
Chambersburg PA
CBHW080331270326
41927CB00014B/3175